VIDEOCASSETTE TECHNOLOGY IN AMERICAN EDUCATION

VIDEOCASSETTE TECHNOLOGY IN AMERICAN EDUCATION

George N. Gordon
Hofstra University
and
Irving A. Falk
New York University

Educational Technology Publications
Englewood Cliffs, New Jersey 07632

Printed in the United States of America.

Library of Congress Catalog Card Number: 72-81494.

International Standard Book Number: 0-87778-035-8.

First Printing

To the memories of:
Charlotte Friel,
Abe Gruskin and
Ben Hoffman

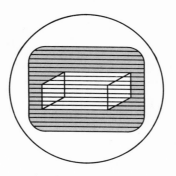

PREFACE

Most books are difficult to start writing; but, between us, the present authors have spawned over a baker's dozen during the past decade in various combinations, with other authors and alone (not to mention "ghost jobs" for politicians and actors). We know the score. The inertia of rest is usually difficult—if not impossible—to overcome in the world of letters.

This volume is different. Starting it was comparatively simple. But it has been almost impossible to *finish.*

The field of videocassette technology is a relatively new one. And daily across our desks flow reams of public relations bulletins, letters, pamphlets, advertisements and newsletters spreading both wide and contradictory news about this electronic miracle that, like the bug in Zeno's paradox, seems to be moving to a goal that is never reached.

This book is *still* unfinished, even at this moment of retrospective introduction, the only sane way to start any literary effort. The next mail will certainly contain data that should have been included in this document but will not be, because one has to stop every project somewhere and at some time. This is the place and the moment! But time, as Henry

Luce once reminded us, marches on. And because our volume is finished, neither the first nor the last word about our topic has been uttered with anything resembling finality within these pages. "Sufficient," says the Good Book, "unto the day is the evil thereof."

This is the day, and the evil is extenuated in the pages that follow.

Words like "revolution," "innovation" and "reform" have somehow been bleached to nothingness in recent educational literature. So we shall not insult the reader's intelligence with the momentous and grand news that the technology of the videocassette will somehow save the Republic and cure athlete's foot. Those of us who have spent our lives in school as teachers and administrators know, if nothing else, deep in our hearts, two brutal truths that fifteen hundred years of educational revolution, reform and innovation have taught our breed: First, teaching is a difficult art (and art it is, although it pays its respects to science) that, like most human affairs, always falls short of its own objectives. Second, there is no *essential* method to pedagogy. Teaching and learning include a varied range of activities, and, accordingly, admit of no absolutely fundamental techniques, systems or combination of systems to educate the young or the old.

The entire history of schooling constitutes a brave, beautiful and praiseworthy attempt to deny these two irrefutable maxims. This total record of dissent has produced some magnificent heat, a little light and many sparks. But the hard truth remains. All education boils down to self-education. Teaching, as we like to think of it, is not difficult, merely impossible—a mystique, actually, forever incorporating into itself a host of intellectual and psychological games and ploys. And last, schools are not necessarily the best places for people to learn things. In fact, and in all probability, they have *not,* for most of us, been the places where we have learned most of the genuinely important things we know in life.

In the light of this realism, to assault the reader at this point with purple prose concerning the role of videocassettes in tomorrow's education would be both futile and silly. Videocassettes are coming—just as movies, TV and sound recording came—into our classrooms on all levels of education, in one way or another. The main question now centers on one proposition alone: *What are we going to do with them?*

First, we have to know what form they are likely to take and what their capabilities and limitations are likely to be. To this end the first chapters of this book are devoted, qualified by the difficulties the reader will soon encounter in our description of a technology that is still early (in all probability) in the process of being developed.

Second, we must attempt to draw up an agenda concerning the reasonable use of this as yet unknowable cassette technology in our various schools as they function today and are likely to operate tomorrow. Considerable guesswork is involved in these projections, of course, because we have had to deal not only with an inchoate technology but also with an institution, the American school, that is forever in transition and, as we have noted, forever being subjected to innovation, revaluation and reform—not to mention its extraordinary heterogeneity.

We honestly expect to be proven dead wrong in some of the considerations that follow, and we admit freely to our peculiar enthusiasms, biases and *amours propres,* both in educational and technological matters, considering our collective experience for three quarters of a century as augurers, teachers, writers and students of one sort or another. We also anticipate that we shall be dead right in others.

This book is being published both too early and too late. It is too early to project fully the potential impact of so ingenious an invention as videocassettes upon education, for the reasons noted above. It is too late to demand of this new technology, *before it has taken on its essential configurations,* those specific requirements that educators might require of it, were they able to sit down with its inventors and engineers and initiate its growth *carte blanche.* In effect, we have been forced, therefore, to straddle these two worlds—successfully, we hope, for the most part.

Our thanks go to Anna Friedman and Mary Brophy for their secretarial skills in the preparation of this manuscript and to Larry Lipsitz of *Educational Technology Publications* for feeding us data and putting up with our insanities in his quiet way. The many errors you will find, particularly in the technical data that follow, are to some degree our fault. But most such inaccuracies result from problems of timing and recording changes in a volatile industry—and from the cold fact that most public relations personnel who work for "get-rich-quick" conglomerates are, almost to a man, damn liars.

Otherwise, we stand by our follies.

George N. Gordon
Irving A. Falk

May, 1972

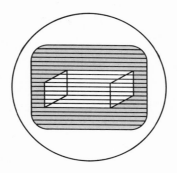

CONTENTS

VIDEOCASSETTE TECHNOLOGY IN AMERICAN EDUCATION

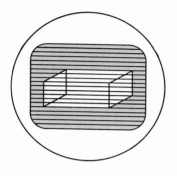

CHAPTER ONE

VIDEOCASSETTES: GENIES OR DEMONS?

Destiny has seen fit to visit upon our culture a paradox: the simple fact that contemporary technology bestows mixed blessings—that for every advance forward in the "know-how" of modern life, one or two dodges sideways are required; sometimes, a step or two backwards.

Whatever happens on the large canvas of society is replicated in miniature in our schools, more swiftly, it seems today, than we were once taught in our Temples of Education. The old myth about schools running, in terms of cultural innovation, about a generation behind the rest of society has had its tenure in the storehouse of American "common wisdom." It is now common nonsense.

At a recent conference on the *industrial* (mind you!) uses of videocassettes in Europe and America—and such conferences are held about once a month these days—executives from the big software and hardware manufacturers in Europe and the United States were agreed on *one* matter only: the marketplace for this new and, perhaps, revolutionary technology will be, first, in the world of education! If, and when, educators figure out how to utilize this remarkable innovation, they both implied and stated, *then* they envision a meeting of videocassette technology with present open-circuit television distribution systems, cable television systems, and even the motion picture distribution business in the rest of society. Only one demur was heard, and that from a British educator whose comments were coated more with whimsy than either vitriol or sugar.

Whether or not the Communications Establishment will succeed in foisting the plans for their new gadgetry on educators is another matter. Too many diversions—and chances for a fast dollar—may obscure their objectives. However, the spirit of their intent is clear: a new technology (or a new version of a couple of old ones) is presently peeping over the horizon. Rather than burden an already saturated culture with a possibly revolutionary type of video instrumentation, the inventors, manufacturers and distributors of this technology are looking at the schools as the first—and most immediately formidable—testing-ground for their wares. Like good businessmen, they have surveyed their potential markets and have found what they think is a soft spot in the underbelly of one of them. What they *cannot* appreciate, because they are quite tone deaf to the elegant cacophony that is emerging from educational quarters these days, is that their tiny soft spot leads directly to the chaos of a dissonantly orchestrated institution: the modern school—lower, middle, high and higher.

The simple fact the electronic executives do not perceive is that their new technology is about to descend into a cultural institution whose deep roots are in considerable tangles. Their instrumentation is on its way into one of the most volatile segments of contemporary culture and will immediately also become *impedimenta* of that volatility.

This has, of course, been the story of *all* technology in education. And one may include here the textbooks, blackboards, school busses and hot lunches.

From a broad perspective, schools generate faithful microcosms of the philosophy, economy and cultural tonus of a given society at a given time. This is the moral of Lawrence Cremin's brilliant monograph, *The Genius of American Education.* The issues that Cremin dealt with were political and social for the most part, but they might have been technological. Technology itself, it seems, is never independent of the *Zeitgeist* of the society in which it operates, or even of the *sub-Zeitgeist* of the particular institution *within which* it operates. Thus, while the videocassette executives are seeking to sidestep the uncertainties of the "consumer market," they seem unaware that they are headed directly into the whirlwinds of conflicting and antagonistic educational philosophies and methods.

In considering the future of videocassettes in American education, then, we are faced with two problems: "What is the technology?" and "What are the educational antagonisms?" It is difficult to decide which to attempt to answer first, because they are not independent one of the other, nor is either a stable enough entity at this writing to describe better than cursorily.

The answer to the first question is, on its face, easier to guess at than the second. At its ultimate peak of inventive perfection (an event we cannot anticipate, we guess, until at least 1975), videocassette technology will duplicate, almost exactly, audiocassette technology—with the addition that color images that move will accompany what are, at present, mere sounds. What this adds up to is, in effect, a cheap and relatively foolproof method of storing "movies" (in their broadest construction) on cassettes derived from one of three sources: (1) central software distributors, like film distributors, for instance; (2) open-circuit or cable television; and/or (3) original home-made television or film productions. These stored programs may then be used ad-lib—in any manner a teacher chooses—in a classroom, their image reconstituted on a television screen or its equivalent, by 1975, that is.

But there is a rub—many rubs, in fact. One much-touted videocassette system (EVR) already exists (but has been consigned both by its inventors and marketers, apparently, to obsolesence at an early age) that can perform all of the functions above *except* #3. Processing must be accomplished by a central service, much as cinema films have always been to date. Numerous educators have therefore observed that this particular process—or any one similar to it—is a software trap, restricting its user to "prepared educational materials." (Accordingly, we begin to hear sounds of educational antagonisms in the distance.) "All the process amounts to," said a not-too-impressed teacher at a demonstration of so-called Electronic Video Recording, "is another way of showing movies. What's the matter with a movie projector?" Begging her final question, her penultimate observation is more or less correct, modified merely by a few practical and financial considerations.

Japanese and European electronic firms are unquestionably in the process of adding function #3, *the ability to make homemade videocassettes,* to the cassette facilities of systems like the dying EVR. (The ultimate instrument may or may not use video *tape* as we know it; one contender is involved in a process employing discs, and another is quietly experimenting with cheap plastic and laser beams.) Some American firms are moving in the same direction. The specific technologies involved are not particularly significant; the direction in which they are leading *is*. It is towards a videocassette system that will, to be brutally frank, permit educators to accomplish at least three ends: to utilize existing and new professional software more simply and conveniently than present methods allow; to permit the same kind of small-time plagiarism that presently occurs almost ubiquitously of printed materials in *all* schools and colleges (by means of Xerography and similar processes) in order to extend its ambit to televised material and movies distributed by open-circuits and cables; and to facilitate the cheap, easily erasable and near-foolproof origination of local "home movie"-type television production, in color, with sound, and as required.

Trailing behind this technology, naturally, are the vested interests of software companies, the entire educational film industry and copyright laws (and the reasonable pragmatic limits of their application). But technology, as recent events in tape sound recording and print reproduction have shown, moves hell-bent-for-leather. And those who are adaptable to its in-built imperatives not only survive, but thrive, on what to others are pitfalls, dangers and threats of ruin.

Plagiarism, for instance (in defiance of copyright laws), of disc sound recordings onto sound tape is, today, one of the most frequent crimes committed indoors in the United States. While it has upset some stable aspects of the recording market, it has also somehow fattened unbelievably the bankrolls of those who moaned—not so long ago—that they would soon be ruined by it. So much, then, for these problems. They are unforeseeable in nature, unpredictable in consequence, and best worried over by the people who will have to live with them.

Videocassette technology, granting time for in-fighting and trial-and-error bouts with the compatibilities of the various systems as they are marketed or developed in prototype, will arrive in the world of formal education at about the time the "educational antagonisms" (the topic of our second question) change from today's sniper forces into battalions, companies and platoons.

Like neutered and spayed cats, educators go through the motions of fighting, and they growl and meow a lot, but they rarely hurt each other. Nature and nurture have insulated academic society from exercising its destructive potential against itself by means of the "greater moralities" all educators think they serve: the transmission of tradition and the amelioration of virtually all our social illnesses. In short, all schoolmen invariably take a stand firmly against vice, and in this grand effort they are indeed united.

They skirmish, however. And the burgeoning gavotte— that should take a few years to heat up—will pit proponents of what might be called "systematic" education against advocates of "informal" education. In short, the former are overt or covert behaviorists who would, disclaimers notwith- standing, rigidify educational procedures along the lines of systems engineering in order to enhance the efficiency of what they believe is, at present, a wasteful way of accom- plishing what they understand as the objectives of schooling. The latter, also in short, are proponents of a more or less unstructured, anti-disciplinary approach to education as "discovery," bespeaking little more concrete in heuristic terms than a high-minded and well-meant *tsimmis* of en- counter therapy, progressivism *a la* the great age of Dewey, a little psychological theory from Freud in paperback and soundings from Piaget.

If the advocates of this great educational argument have been slightly caricatured in the paragraph above, the exagger- ation is justified by the ardor of some (but not all) of their enthusiasts. The "systemists" at their worst (or best) are caricature twentieth century positivists: all method, bound by flowcharts, quantifying, measuring and manipulating in a world of "inputs," "sequences" and "outputs." The "informalists" are just as bizarre: they cosset a sentimental vision of play-therapy extended to teaching algebra and history, with teacher as guru, possessed of (or blessed by) some transcendental educational design that salvages meaning from the abolition of authority—both personal and intellectual—in an epistemological universe so relative that even Einstein's mathematics will not contain it. It operates on faith, less in science or democracy than in the natural perfection of Edgar Rice Burroughs' uncorrupted ape-man.

Historians of education might call our educational confrontation an ancient "tension" using new *impedimenta,* and, to a degree, they would be right. For at least seventy-five years, in America, "formalists" have been at the jugulars of "informalists" and vice-versa, not only in children's schools but in medical academies, agricultural institutes, dance studios and barbers' colleges. The positions of both are exacerbating and hardening today, however, because neither is apparently as free as they once were of many searching and fundamental questions concerning social, economic and ontological assumptions that young people, mostly, have hurled in the faces of their elders during the past decade. These questions are being posed today in the matrix of the deepest cultural crisis we have yet experienced in our history, a crisis, ironically, born of the historical curiosity that our nation has not had to face a *real* crisis (and therefore put aside our ongoing animosities) for the past generation.

As Henry J. Perkinson observed in *The Imperfect Panacea: American Faith in Education, 1865-1965,* the schools have been called upon continuously to serve as anodynes for society's problems and have continually failed to deliver. Agricultural schools, vocational schools, professional schools, integrated schools, open-enrollment schools, authoritarian schools, free-wheeling elective schools and aristocratic Ivy-League schools—all have responded in their ways to the needs of American society, and all have brought forth far from perfect solutions. Perhaps too much has been expected of them: enhancement of society's traditional values, advancement of our technological know-how, breakthroughs in pure and applied knowledge, amelioration of our volatile and shifting ethnic and social arrangements, as well as issuing of credentials of certification to masses of students in order to allow them to qualify for practice in society as teachers, doctors, lawyers and the like. This multi-purposed role of the schools has brought into and out of vogue aspects of "systemic" and aspects of "informal" education off and on through the history of American society in undulating cycles.

We have even come to the point now where Ivan Illich advocates an advance into anarchy for curing society's ills. The solution is embodied thematically in the title of his recent book: *Deschooling Society.* What Illich has accomplished merely extenuates the "informalist" point of view *ad absurdum.* While Perkinson and others think that the schools, called upon to solve society's problems, have come up with imperfect solutions, Illich postulates that *too* much emphasis is placed upon schooling in America and that in this emphasis lies the core of many of our problems. Hence, he advocates "deschooling America." Illich has merely carried the "informalist" point of view forward along the anarchistic track of the anti-institutionalist, whose thesis is that all institutions are destructive of independence; that institutionalism, in any form, renders the student passive and thus only superficially receptive to the values of education. He advocates breaking up the institution of the school and substituting for it various kinds of active relationships of personal encounters to combat institutional boredom, suggesting the creation of "opportunity webs" (in place of schools) in which students have access to educational objects, skill exchanges, peer-watching, educators-at-large, libraries, factories, farms, museums and storefront depots. Of course, this kind of educational smorgasbord must, in time, also evolve into its *own kind of institutionalized relationships* and inherit the evils thereof, thus completing this cycle of recreating that which it set out to destroy.

If, in other words, our main educational problem in schooling is to create people, and not mere *personnel*, out of students, neither the "formalists" nor the "informalists" have yet found adequate answers that lead anywhere but back to the problem.

So where does the humble technology of videorecording—and particularly the videocassette—fit into this broad and possibly insoluble set of antagonisms? In other words, how does the technology relate to the confrontation of "systemists" versus "informalists"? Or does it?

Everything, of course, that happens in education relates to the confrontation. Whatever educational procedure is continued, discontinued or introduced into our schools will immediately become engulfed in the methodological assumptions by which those schools operate, and the ambit of this fact is wide enough to cover prayers at assembly, varsity football and new swimming pools.

Videocassette technology, however, the ultimate (to date) in recording instrumentation, is an important procedure (by no means revolutionary but important) *both* to "systematized" and to "informal" education. Back in the 1950s, a hyperbolic administrator at New York University made a frequently quoted prediction that television would shortly become the most important educational instrument since the invention of the textbook. Well, he was wrong, and has since gone on to administrative greatness.

Videocassette technology, on the other hand, *may* turn out to be *as useful* as any or all other educational aids invented to date. But it may *not* as well, depending less upon its own technological development than the kinds of experiences in school we are going to call "educational" during the next generation. The judgment we must make in answer to this possibility, if we are to avoid the error of NYU's haruspex, will depend, in fact, upon what direction schooling in America takes, and the options are multiple—two at base but compounded in numerous permutations and combinations.

First, videocassettes fit neatly into nearly all "systems," and are therefore likely to become beloved *impedimenta* of the "systemists." To meet their rigid educational requirements, the kind of cassettes they will favor (just as they favor similar "frames" in programmed instruction and atomized lesson components) will be those of the type already available—that is, prepared, tested, professional, certified, validated and (probably) standardized jots of educational software that will fit into their systems. If we may judge the future of this software by that of the past, most of it is likely to be neither inspired nor inspiring—mixing, as it does, the product "know-how" of educational film makers (in most cases, educational illiteracy) with Kodachrome ineptitude. Such software, also, because it is standardized, cannot meet the special and distinctive needs created in every different sort of educational situation. Teachers know that, even when systematizing their basic procedures, nearly every class, school or section of a course of study is in some manner distinctive.

This software—and here may be its most deadly peril—also becomes dated with amazing rapidity. "Knowledge," wrote A.N. Whitehead, "does not keep any better than fish," and no one since his pronouncement has figured out how to put a lesson or demonstration, even a short chemistry lesson, in a deep-freeze. There will always be a newer, and presumably better, way to perform or teach it than the one presently in use—with exceptions. If the systems of the "systemists" are to keep up to date, they will develop a merciless tapeworm for software—one that it may not be possible to feed.

The "informalists" will not be too interested in this pre-fab software, except as a way to keep their liberated students from *excessive* liberation, and as an occasional way to teach them something that they did not "discover" themselves—when faced with the call for a progress report from administrators or parents. At times of such crises, the informalists are likely to grab any software in the broom closet out of desperation, along, possibly, with a few student workbooks and kits of programmed instruction.

What the informalists will find most interesting—and attractive—is the potential of videocassette technology for them and their students to do their "thing." One's "thing" is a critical byword of contemporary culture, and its nebulous haze presently follows one from cradle to grave. The word "thing" is apt; vocabulary follows custom with a bee-line. A "thing" is formless, timeless, valueless and protean. It is as relevant to kindergarten *Katzenjammers* as to the quasi-political ravings of a law professor out to "green" America. It is—must be—informal, unless your "thing" is formality, in which case you are surrounded by others for whom the prescribed "thing" is nondirective, and you feel like an idiot.

A "thing" also comes out of the self. *If* there is nothing in the self, nothing comes out, and having "done it," one is back where one started, a not infrequent eventuality of educational procedures (one hesitates to call them "classes" or "seminars") involving empty students and vapid teachers—little or big—doing silly "things" in the name of education.

Videocassette technology, in whatever form it takes, *as long as that form permits a recording facility,* is likely to become *the essential instrument* of informal education (rather than an ancillary aid, as to structural education), and this is not a prediction by a university administrator out to get his name in the newspaper. It is a condition of tomorrow's education, if the informalists dictate the nature and direction of tomorrow's American schooling. At this point in history, it honestly and realistically looks as if they may, for better or worse.

This new (or renewed) technology has the power to turn *all aspects* of schooling—and some aspects of teaching as we have grown to understand it—*inwards.* In other words, relatively cheap and easy videorecording is best understood as a means of expression in cognitive *or* affective domains, as you will, for teachers and students to do their "thing." In this respect, it is consonant with the *modi operandorum* of *both* "structural" and "informal" education in many significant ways. But, just as it serves as a means of expression for instruction of any type—good or bad, disciplined or unstructured—it is also a powerful means for students of all ages to (a) do their "thing," whatever it is, and (b) observe themselves doing their "thing"—and allowing them to audit it, observe it, laugh at it, cry at it and (hopefully) learn from it.

At its best, think of the all-too-obvious uses of

videocassette instant-playback in speech therapy or reading practice for small children. Or, in mode (b) above, consider moot trials in law schools that may be scrutinized, criticized, analyzed, or played back, having segments repeated and stopped on a frame, a word, a gesture or point of procedure or law. At its worst, imagine home-brewed videocassette lessons of the general quality of commercial ITV software repeated *ad nauseam* to section after section of social studies students year after year. Or, again in the second mode, a term project on the Civil War re-enacted on videotape in place of an essay in English by a high school senior who requires training in the decorum of written communications and the fundamentals of historical research.

Whatever its destiny, videocassette technology has emerged with its distinctive potentials—far more interesting and directly applicable to our current concepts of education than mere "television," which is, after the grand disillusionment of two and one-half decades, just a quick way of showing and distributing talks, newsreels, movies and sales pitches—at a critical moment in the history of our schools. That it will be drawn into the vortex of the educational maelstrom is almost certain, more predictably than the destiny of other instruments of educational technology on the scene today, including computers, programs, conventional films, allied hardware and any other kind of software of which one can conceive. In a way, it is a *sleeper,* not unlike its older but smaller brother, the audiocassette—that has, in a quiet way, revised a culture's relationship towards the spontaneous and recorded nature of sound and human speech. Should videocassette technology, in fact, influence directively both the tempo and direction of that twister, do not be surprised. But—like all technology—new "know-how" and new instrumentation do not necessarily yield progress. All they guarantee is *change.*

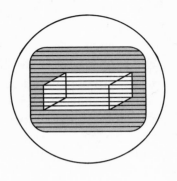

CHAPTER TWO

THINKING TAPE

The exquisite depth of the naiveté of some educators should not surprise anyone who has spent more than an hour in a contemporary palace of learning—at least, if he or she is over thirty.

A short time ago a female professor seated herself in the office of a director of communications at a respectable university and asked if it might be possible for him to arrange for the showing of a film a colleague at another university had made for her class.

The director, suspicious of anyone who knows anyone who makes films, inquired what sort of film it was.

"Oh, TV film," replied the lady professor. "Professor X makes them all the time. All I want to do is show it in my class."

"TV film! Do you mean 8mm, Super 8, 16mm or 35mm, sound or silent, optical or magnetic track?"

The professor nodded. "Yes. I think she said it was Japanese. It's a film in which she shows how Piaget works with children."

"Do you have the film with you?" asked the director.

At this the professor reached into her knitting bag. "Here! She said I could use it as long as I wanted."

The director received into his hand a box of one-inch magnetic videotape. He looked at it, smelled it and tapped it with his forefinger. The reel was bare of information of any sort except an obscure brand name and the word PIAGET written by a Magic Marker. He proceeded cautiously.

"What you have here, my dear, is *videotape*—not a film. Do you have any idea what sort of instrument was used for recording it? The maker, the model—any morsel of information about its origin?"

The professor smiled at what she now regarded obviously as the director's mental obtuseness and genius for irrelevance.

"I want to show it at 4 o'clock." (It was then 3:30.) "I don't see what the trouble is. You show films all the time for other classes, don't you? The class next to mine had Walter Cronkite Tuesday night. He made so much noise I could hardly hear my own voice."

The scene that followed was nasty enough to draw a discreet curtain upon, but it has been played—and is being played—in multitudinous variations today across the United States. It has been stimulated by hyperthyroid advertising and teachers hankering to produce "cheap and dirty" films of their unique teaching methods and other trivia on portable video instruments—to have something to show their colleagues at conventions or as homework for their graduate classes. Videorecording, others think, is *the* relevant and logical alternative to assignments involving print, photographs or other so-called media. Television taping, in the minds of many, is also synonymous with the facile *sound* recording today permitted by battery-powered cartridge instruments.

To others, it is construed as a versatile version of home-movie gear, or an easy way to pirate movies, educational television programs or news broadcasts from the air or community antenna systems for home or classroom use. To still others, videorecording (or some version of it) holds out a promise of relegating Super 8 and 16mm sound film to oblivion by means of various cassette and cartridge devices yet to be invented and marketed—and so on and so on and so on.

Most of the mythology above is, at the present moment of the state of development of the art of using videotape, sheer moonshine, reflecting half-truths, exaggerated salesmanship and the literary efforts of ill-named "forward-looking" enthusiasts who are attempting to reverse the old (and untrue) cliché that schooling in America runs about a generation behind the rest of culture by kicking it mindlessly a quarter of a century *into the future.* They are all victims, not of "future shock," but of "futuristic neurosis" and of science fiction mentalities, blind to the exciting possibilities of the present moment, because they are too busy living in their dreams of tomorrow.

A bit of history is therefore in order:

Videotape and videotaping procedures are a remarkable culmination of technological progress in three fields: optics, sound recording and magnetic electronics. Following the invention of photography, pioneers in cinema introduced various forms of controlled mechanical motion to sequences of still pictures that resulted in an illusion of optical motion. Curiously, at about the same time, mechanical motion was also employed to recreate sounds caused by a vibrating needle moving within grooves on a rotating cylinder. What we may loosely call "talking movies" were therefore invented about three generations ago. (The first films were, indeed, synchronized to crude phonographs, and many of them, incidentally, were shown in color.) At the heart of this primitive system of reconstituting sound and picture, therefore, was mechanical motion, often provided by a hand crank or spring mechanism. Mechanical motion remains fundamental to *all* methods of recreating sounds and moving pictures used today, even the most sophisticated.

What changed—or was modified—in time were recording methods and sources and types of mechanical motion. Sound recording had a colorful history: from wax cylinders to wax, metal, acetate and plastic discs—to the microgroove 33 1/3 rpm recording we know today, as well as optical methods of recording sound tracks on film, the method used in most sound movie systems. Sound on film techniques also anticipated wire recording and modern sound tape devices. Photo-electric sound recording remains an excellent way of preserving voices and music, incidentally, but one which requires photo processing, like movie film. From this procedure the notion of achieving the mechanical motion necessary for recording (and playback) by means of passing a recorded strip of ribbon from reel to reel emerged, a modification that had been used for many years by instruments involving pictures in motion.

As most high school students know, the development of wire and, later, iron oxide and chromium dioxide tape and tape recorders permitted the storage of sound "information" (an engineering misnomer in common usage) without producing a physical change in the wire or tape itself. Sound was stored in the pattern of alignment of electrons in the tape and, passing an electronic field, disturbed that field and translated it into sound vibrations electronically instead of mechanically, as in conventional disc recordings.

At this point in the history of modern technology a fascinating question arose. If sound information could be stored in this peculiar way on oxide tape, might pictorial information be stored there also? The answer was clearly "no," as long as the pictures were photographic and optical. *But,* if pictures might somehow be transferred into electronic impulses . . .

Along came TV, which, of course, accomplished precisely this: the translation of a visual field into a stream of electrons. (Mechanical motion was not needed for this process, nor is it presently needed as long as the electronic picture is instantaneously transmitted or "live." As soon as a picture is stored, its reconstitution requires mechanical motion.) That stream of electrons might then be fed into oxide tape (wider tape than generally used for sound recording because more information was stored) and, lately, tape coated with chromium dioxide, and the result was sound- and videorecording.

Neither the invention of videorecording nor the theory involved in its development was either this pat, logical or simple, of course. Accident, error and necessity are all mothers of invention. Two major problems arose as the result of this latter technological advance, however, and they now seem inevitable in the light of our capsule history. First, enormous amounts of information had to be stored on the oxide tape to handle sound and electronically control the various signals and pictures in black and white and color resolved on a television tube. The storage process had to be both extremely precise and complex. Second, enormously rapid mechanical motion was also required to reconstitute this galaxy of electronic impulses. Roughly speaking, the wider the tape, the slower these speeds might be in order to receive, store and reproduce the requisite information with fidelity.

The first professional videotape recorders introduced

during the nineteen-fifties into the broadcasting industry (and the ancestors of the sophisticated color instruments in use there today) were called *quadriplex* or *transverse* recorders. They stored their electronic information on tape 2 inches wide in a vertical pattern. These professional broadcast instruments produced an exceptionally sophisticated electronic picture and were both large in size and extremely expensive, serving the needs of professional broadcasters. Their grandchildren used in the big broadcasting studios are equally complex. They have little (if any) relevance to the kind of equipment most useful for videotaping in schools. Nor may tapes recorded on quadriplex instruments be played back on any of the smaller, cheaper and more flexible recorders generally used for non-broadcast purposes, unless they are first re-recorded onto a tape size and electronic format compatible with these less sophisticated instruments.

Most videorecorders useful for school purposes employ *helical scan* procedures for storing information on tape; that is, electronic information is placed on the magnetic tape in a series of minute, more or less parallel, diagonal lines. They are, in effect, jammed into the tape as economically as possible, along with pulses to control the stability of the eventually reconstituted image, as well as one or two sound tracks. Regardless of the type of recorder, thirty frames (or individual pictures per second) are recorded (and played back) at normal speed. Rotating recording heads and the speed the tape runs from reel to reel produce sufficient mechanical motion (many, many times faster than the speed of movie film running through an optical projector) to extract this enormous amount of electronic information from the magnetized particles in the tape.

Tape width, once again, is a function of the tape's storage capacity. And most helical scan recorders—or those with the widest educational applications—employ either 1, 1/2, or 1/4 inch tape.

Obviously, 1 inch videorecorders are usually able to produce somewhat sharper images and store more electronic information than 1/2 inch recorders; and the latter are generally superior to 1/4 inch recorders in this respect. A trained eye will notice these differences: clarity of image, stability of picture, contrast, visibility of details and other minutiae that the layman may miss in the replayed image. But they may be important at times for certain esoteric educational purposes: recognizing numbers on football players' uniforms, for instance.

On the other hand, 1/2 inch recorders are cheaper and less bulky, by and large, than 1 inch instruments, and frequently produce pictures of surprising clarity, crispness and stability, if they are used properly.

Quarter-inch recorders have been on the "fringes" of the VTR market for many years, and recently a well-made Japanese instrument using this tape size has been introduced to the American market. Although it employs considerable lengths of tape for information storage, it is unquestionably the most compact videorecorder on the market today, and the images and sound the authors examined while inspecting the instrument were of consistently good quality. The 1/4 inch instruments are also quite reasonably priced—in the $1,000-$1,500 range, comparable to 1/2 inch recorders—without accessory equipment in both cases.

Awareness of the types of recorders and the tape sizes they use does not tell the whole story of videorecording, of course. A VTR, unlike a motion picture camera or phonograph, is *both* an instrument for recording and storing pictures and sounds *as well as* a device for playing them back. Both functions require auxiliary equipment. (At present, some new video-playback machines for various types of cartridges, discussed below, are designed only to play back prerecorded materials in a number of ways.) This auxiliary equipment falls into two classes: (1) origination equipment employed to place the video and audio signals on tape and (2) playback equipment by which these signals are made audible and visible on a video tube.

We, therefore, arrive at the fundamental problem of our communications center director who faced the earnest professor on the first page of this chapter. Obviously, material stored on 1 inch, 1/2 inch or 1/4 inch tape must be played back on VTRs designed for their own tape width. *But the problem of compatibility goes beyond this.* By and large, VTR tapes may only be played back (with any degree of fidelity) on instruments using the same general electronic scansion format as the instruments on which they were recorded or duplicated, meaning usually, instruments of the same manufacturer's "line" and "model series." In fact, it is safe to state that any individual 1 inch, 1/2 inch or 1/4 inch TV tape will probably be most satisfactorily played back on the *identical* instrument which recorded it (or its twin). Both electronic functions and mechanical speeds will be identical with the conditions of their recording. In helical scan recording, this matter of instrument-to-instrument compatibility is as important as (or more important than, if tapes are to be transported for playback to instruments other than those used for recording) the subtle capacities of certain models to store more or less electronic information on tape, or the degree of sharpness of picture and fidelity of sound.

Our director's problem was, therefore, not centered on the size of the tape the professor had given him: he immediately saw that it could only be played back on a 1 inch VTR. The questions he could not answer were on what make, brand and model VTR the recording had been made, whether he possessed a compatible instrument in his stock, or whether the material on the tape had been recorded in black and white or color. Even if he might procure a supposedly compatible instrument, whether or not he would be able to produce an acceptable playback might well be simply a matter of chance determined by many conditions under which the tape was originally recorded. The professor's naiveté notwithstanding, he had quite a job ahead of him in determining all of these variable factors from a reel of unmarked oxide and plastic tape.

Helical scan VTRs differ from one another in many ways, tape width being only one of them. The differences relate mostly to the number of "extra features" they employ, each one of which allows the operator to achieve different types of effects in both recording and editing videotape.

Electronic editing features are perhaps the most important, allowing one to achieve the same sort of effects on videotape as a film editor may achieve when splicing film. Two VTRs are required to take full advantage of electronic editing. In effect, various short videotaped segments may be fed from instrument to instrument, the second one (or "second generation," as engineers say) containing in sequence—and with suitable "fades," "dissolves" and "wipes" in fancy editing—a final tape made up of sequences from one or more other tapes, cut and arranged in proper order.

The number of audio tracks on a VTR tape is also significant, if one wants to add commentary, music or sound effects to tapes after they have been completed. This "audio overdubbing" is only possible in instruments employing a dual sound track system.

Color VTRs are currently available in the 1 inch and 1/2 inch tape formats. In all instances, they may be used to record in black and white (using black and white cameras) and will usually play back tapes made on similar instruments (make and model). They are, for the most part, much more expensive than black and white VTRs.

Slow motion and "still frame" capacities are other VTR features. The latter allows one, in playback, to halt a picture on a single "frame" or picture. (In fact, the instrument simply continues reconstituting the same electronic information from a small segment of tape over and over again.) In the former instance, the normal rate of "frame production" of a videotape—thirty per second in all television broadcasting—is reduced to produce a slow-motion effect similar to that achieved on movie film, by increasing the number of frames projected per second to slow down optical action. In this latter instance, optics and electronics work in exactly opposite ways to achieve an identical effect.

As far as prices of VTRs are concerned, they vary widely, according to the sophistication of the instrumentation, *not* according to the size of tape they employ. A low-priced, reasonably simple 1 inch VTR is considerably less expensive than a complex color 1/2 inch one. The highest priced helical scan instrument on the market today (about $12,500) uses 1 inch tape because it can do more with the wider tape than the most expensive 1/2 inch instruments (about $1,500). Prices, however, for most VTRs range from $700 to $5,000, excluding some of the more elaborate and sophisticated instruments of American manufacture. The least expensive VTRs, incidentally, are presently of Japanese origin and compare favorably with American and European instruments in regard to price and quality. VTR tape itself costs about $60 per hour for 1 inch; $40 per hour for 1/2 inch; and about $25 per hour for 1/4 inch tape. (Conventional 1/4 inch *sound* tape cannot be used for present 1/4 inch

VTRs.)

Equipment required for *origination* of VTR tapes may likewise be held to simple and inexpensive instruments or, if complex production is required, may take on elaborate and expensive proportions. The essential piece of originating apparatus, of course, is the TV camera, which employs a *vidicon* tube that relays picture information, either directly to a VTR instrument or to a *switcher* and/or *processing amplifier* if more than one camera is used. If multiple cameras are employed, it is also necessary to feed them electronically to the cameras from a single *synchronizing generator* that provides an even and steady electronic pulse so that, when pictures are switched from camera to camera, they will remain stable and not jump or seem to break apart. The sync generator provides the *sync pulse* on which these cameras operate evenly.

In videorecording, most vidicon cameras, with slight modification, may be made to work with any 1 inch or 1/2 inch VTR instrument. Prices of cameras depend upon their electronic sophistication, the nature of the viewfinder they use (electronic or optical) and the amount of ancillary equipment they contain—usually so-called EIA processors, which bring the quality of the picture up to certain standards. They range in price, in monochrome, from about $250 to $35,000; and a color camera may cost about $7,000 to $15,000 for helical scan recording. Cameras require lenses and, until comparatively recently, various lenses with different focal lengths (often from 25mm to 150mm) were mounted over a camera aperture on a turret. More recently, however, zoom lenses have replaced the turret, because they are able to change focal lengths easily and smoothly, either by manual or electronic control mechanisms. A ten-to-one zoom lens may achieve all focal lengths that lenses from

12mm to 120mm might provide on a turret, while a five-to-one zoom may range (in a single shot) from a 20mm (medium wide angle) to a 100mm (medium telephoto) picture in a single camera shot.

Cameras and monitoring systems do not operate in a manner similar to optical cameras in *one* main respect: the image that is taped, or reconstituted on a video tube, is made up of dots that are distributed into rapidly arranged lines of light and dark signals. In optical cameras, waves of light containing a *whole* picture are chemically recorded on a full frame surface, a different matter entirely.

Most TV picture "frames" (a given picture at a given instant) consist of approximately 525 such lines in the USA, but they may be distributed on the tube in different linear sequences, known as "interlaces." Relatively crude TV cameras operate in *random* interlace; that is, the pattern of lineation (and picture resolution) is left more or less to chance. (Oddly, highly sophisticated *color* TV systems also interlace at random, but the addition of color information to black and white information produces a picture of considerable clarity and fine definition.) Some more sophisticated black and white cameras utilize a *2:1 interlace* pattern; the spread of lines across the tube is controlled in such a way that alternate lines are predictably reconstituted on the tube face. So-called EIA-broadcast standard synchronization, which regulates closely all the pulse generation in a VTR system, will hold the image from camera to VTR and/or monitors to the rigid 2:1 interlace pattern and thereby usually achieve video pictures of high quality, although the introduction of such equipment is only necessary for video recording when multiple cameras and switching and/or a special effects generator is also employed in the system—or in case tapes are to be broadcast on open TV channels.

Equipment for reconstituting (or displaying) a VTR picture is less complicated than the many types and variations of originating equipment, the main components of which are indicated above. A VTR recorder in the playback mode must, of course, feed into a *monitor*, which is nothing more than a television receiver fitted (internally or externally) with an RF converter that is attached, in effect, to the antenna leads of the set. The same instrumentation may be employed to display either cable or open-circuit broadcasts received on the monitor if it is attached to the proper antenna or cable outlet. Conventional home receivers may be used as VTR monitors, although instruments especially designed for this purpose usually produce more satisfactory images.

Should one want to reconstitute a VTR program on a number of monitors, a *distribution amplifier* is necessary to amplify and apportion the signal in sufficient electronic potency for each of the monitors. In operation, such an amplifier is the distributing mirror image (or twin) of the previously discussed sync generator that divides and controls electronic pulses in multiple cameras in video origination. In both cases, it is *possible* to operate a VTR system (origination from more than one camera; distribution to more than one monitor) without these signal "quality control" devices, but the results are usually poor quality pictures in most cases, with distorted sound and unpredictable results. Constant, synchronous electronic pulses of stable intensity lie at the heart of any VTR recording or playback facility where more than one camera or monitor are used, or where special effects and/or electronic editing are attempted.

Of considerable importance are the size and weight of VTR recorders and allied equipment. Advertisements frequently imply that VTRs are featherweight, compact and easily transported from place to place: True enough, in some cases, if you own a trained elephant to carry them.

Most 1 inch VTR recorders, "whether," in Oscar Wilde's words, "they have handles on them or not," are heavy—from 40 to 100 pounds. An average 1 inch instrument weighs about fifty pounds. Vidicon cameras weigh anywhere from four to fifty pounds. It is impractical even to think of using a VTR camera that weighs 15 pounds as a "hand-held" instrument. It requires a tripod or some other sort of mount. VTRs using 1/2 inch tape are, in general, not much lighter than 1 inch instruments, the heaviest weighing from 60 to 70 pounds. Half-inch *portable* VTRs (advertised as "feather-weight" in brochures displaying a slim girl in a bathing suit with a VTR over her shoulder and a camera held lightly in her left hand) *are* "portable," but within limits. Such a VTR itself may weigh 19 or 20 pounds, and its camera, six or seven pounds. The lightest set on the market today—a 1/4 inch instrument—weighs about 10 pounds (without tape) and the camera associated with it weighs 4 pounds. Nothing involved in videorecording is "featherweight."

Associated equipment follows the general weight of the equipment it services. A look at a manufacturer's catalog confirms what the layman should already know: that, in recent years, weights of fairly simple electronic equipment (like radios) and mechanical equipment to some degree (like portable phonographs and sound cassette recorders) have been reduced noticeably, but *complicated* electronic equipment combined with motors producing high and precise speeds still tend to be heavy. Even a moderate-sized color TV monitor is, to some degree, portable. But it is heavy, nevertheless, because of its sophisticated components, and its complex electronic adjustments are not improved by moving it around too frequently without tender, loving care.

Another important point in regard to VTR equipment that leads to misunderstanding of its capacities and flexibility is that electronic devices, by and large, while not much heavier in many cases than optical equipment (such as still and motion picture cameras of various kinds), tend to be less rugged and more sensitive to damage from motion, changes in weather, tobacco smoke and ashes and dust—as well as electrical interferences of various kinds—than conventional photographic gear. In short, a VTR camera or recorder *is not* a movie camera (no matter how complex) and must be handled and operated in a different manner from a conventional camera. The only exactly identical elements of VTRs and movie cameras are the lenses both employ. Otherwise, they are different in almost every respect, and they function differently and produce different sorts of results under the same conditions.

Another history lesson is also in order here: The terms "cassettes" and "cartridges" are, these days, used more or less interchangeably by the general public, most of whom have very little idea of what either of them mean—or what they are. This state of affairs is satisfactory as far as manufacturers of these pieces of equipment (or materials) are concerned, because such a wide range of models and types exist. And they work so differently and require such different levels of manufacturing sophistication (to say nothing of the matter of proprietary patents) that the less the public knows about them, they calculate, the better.

Both terms are, in some measures, misnomers and do not describe the objects they presently label. The cartridge's antecedent is familiar and stems directly from military usage, except that the software in the cartridge (or clip) for a rifle, pistol or revolver is expendable. Sound and videotape cartridges re-use their own software or contents, one way or another. The cartridge idea, however, is the same: a gadget that permits sequential use of software without loading—for lethal or non-lethal purposes.

The immediate antecedent of the term "cassette" is found in the world of photography. A cassette is simply a case, and photographers long ago developed film-packs that would ease the loading (like a cartridge of film) into a camera and advance it from one reel to another, as one took a series of pictures. This software was (and is) eventually removed from the cassette for purposes of developing and printing.

If sanity prevailed in our labeling and naming procedures, both audio and video "cassettes" and "cartridges" might now be defined and described in a single paragraph. Sanity does not prevail, but the history of both (whose function, obviously, is not always the same) may explain the reason for the confusion.

With the invention of sound tape, professional broadcasters (its first wide-scale users) were faced with the problem of threading playback instruments with reel-to-reel magnetic tape every time they wanted to use a short announcement that might be repeated twenty times a day. Each time it was aired, it had to be rewound, cued and set for the next playing. Necessity once more mothered invention, and drawn from experiences going back a generation to the world of amusement park film projection, a cartridge was devised that, by cleverly creating an endless loop, would replay (continuously) short announcements, commercials, station-breaks, etc., without rewinding. All you had to do was stop it before it started up again.

To perfect such an endless loop that works efficiently is not as simple as it sounds, incidentally, because it poses a problem in basic physics that goes back to antiquity, involving twisting the tape or film as it comes back for replay so that it is in position to start again. In early movie viewers using the technique, the film also had to slide across itself, and the wear and tear upon it was considerable. The solution was the invention of a cartridge with tracks that protected the film (as used in film cartridges today) or tape in its trip to and from its holding reel.

At about the same time as the cartridge was perfected, a need also arose from individuals (hobbyists, teachers and others) owning conventional tape recorders for an endless loop of much the same kind—some manner of replaying a longer message than those usually used by radio stations, over and over again—perhaps a sales pitch or orientation message, or an endless flow of repeated background music. For this purpose, a cartridge known by its trade name (after the owner of the first patents) appeared on the market. Called the Cousino Cartridge, it could turn any reel-to-reel recorder into an endless loop playback instrument by threading the tape into a special cartridge.

No problem yet. These were all *cartridges*, properly named because of their convenience in loading. They all employed *one* main reel of tape, a spindle to return the tape after it was used and one or another ingenious method of circumventing the ancient physical principle that still applies: a spool of thread cannot be forced into an endless loop and, at the same time, keep all surfaces of the thread in the same relationship they were on the original reel—at least, while the loop is moving. For movie film and tape, the cartridge was and is, in effect, an endless loop that is twisted back upon itself.

Enter, then, the cassette.

The sound-tape cassette was a European invention that, in terms of function, needs no detailed description. Cassette sound recorders are presently ubiquitous, and it seems quite obvious what a sound cassette is and how it works. It is obvious because it is a far *less* sophisticated piece of software than the cartridge that it followed into the world of technology, utilizing a simple principle long familiar to 35mm photography and home movie buffs.

While it presented (and still presents) certain engineering problems of a sticky nature (alignment, balance, tension, etc.), it constitutes, at heart, an extremely elementary device. Containing *two* reels—one to feed and one to take up—the cassette is simply an ingenious way to eliminate the threading problems of reel-to-reel tape recorders (keeping one's grimy hands off the oxide tape) and aligning a thin piece of tape *precisely* with a recording or playback head. It does not bother with endless loops or fundamental problems in physics. When you have finished recording or playing the tape from the feed loop, you must *rewind it*—or flip it over and use the other horizontal half of the tape, thereby rewinding the original half. While these cassettes differ widely in quality, due to the care of manufacture and sophistication of the tiny mechanisms which you do *not* see that control the tension and balance of the tape, they all work in exactly the same way, either poorly or smoothly—for a long or short time.

At this point the matter of terminology—as well as mechanics—seems settled. *Cartridges* involve *one* reel, wound in an endless loop, while *cassettes* involve *two* reels that are not endless. Happy? This principle should now apply to film cartridges, audiotape cassettes, videotape cartridges and so forth.

It should, *but it does not.*

In the first place, with the introduction of various types of video-playback cartridges and cassettes into the theoretical market (only prototypes have been produced in most instances), manufacturers began to get coy. While some have been candid about the matter, others have been so secretive and ambiguous in their press releases and demonstrations that they have purposely confused the terminology of their software in an effort to keep secret the way it *works.* Something called "Cartrivision" operates on a cartridge principle; and so does Electronic Video Recording, although CBS did (until it lost its enthusiasm for its invention) not seem to care what you called its little film packages as long as you used the word "revolutionary" in talking about them. They are not revolutionary; they are cartridges. But what about *Instavision*, a cartridge, although Ampex does not seem fond of the word? Sony's (and other Japanese) videocassettes are true cassettes (two reels), although Victor of Japan (NIVICO) is tinkering, apparently, with a video-cartridge, and various Japanese firms have announced that in addition to videocassettes, they are interested in EVR and other types of tape and film cartridges.

Second, in Cannes, France, at New York University and elsewhere, "Videocassette Conferences," "Seminars" and other diversions have been held, at which most of the instrumentation for videorecording (but not all) has featured cartridges. Speakers at these conferences refer to cartridges and cassettes as if they do not know the difference between the two, which is probably true; and as if they could not care less about the issue, which is also probably the case. Newspaper and magazine writers, even in the trade, are properly confused about the issue, but not noticeably more than both the experts and prophets.

Third, what do you call the little pack, emerging from German technology, that employs a stack of sequential video *discs* which are plunked into a playback machine and result in substantially the same sort of playback as a video-*cartridge*? The pressure pick-up head may or may not go back to the original disc in the stack. The turntable stays in the same place, as do the discs. Is this cartridge or cassette—either, neither or both? Cartridge, probably, but it was described by an enthusiast to the authors as a "disc type, record cassette cartridge," a locution that cannot be faulted too severely.

This issue is hardly a semantic crisis. It is indicative merely (as are all vocabulary and terminological problems) of an *external display of internal confusion.* Our suggestion is to stick to linguistic history and to make sure others do so. In firearms and educational technology, one *uses* a cartridge but does not rewind it; he throws it away or starts again. He may live to reload it. One *plays* (or *records*) a cassette and rewinds it to replay, play or re-record it. In film and tape technology, a *cartridge* employs *one feed reel* and return system; thus the invariable presence of the impossible: the endless loop. A *cassette* sends film or tape from one reel to another and back again, according to both conventional logic and physics. It may contain automatic cut-off devices, alarms and other refinements, but it is a simple reel-to-reel device in a package.

Anything that uses discs, laser beams, old plastic Baggies or paper-toweling should be regarded as a *cartridge* if, following its finish (after it has played its program), it is ready to start up again *without a rewinding procedure* or its equivalent. If it must be reset in more than a cursory way (more complicated than flicking a switch or waiting *one or two seconds*), it should be considered a *cassette.*

Before this revolution in video technology begins, it might be a good idea if we all knew what we were talking about.

To sum up, videotape recording is a distinctive technology. In 1 inch and 1/2 inch formats (particularly as used in schools) it is different from professional, commercial 2 inch transverse videorecording, on one hand, and different—very different—from both sound-tape recording and from movie-making. One learns little about videotape recording procedures in school from watching the way that a broadcast network tapes a variety show or from observing the shooting of a movie. He learns his arts and skills by familiarizing himself with the various capacities—and technological assets and limitations—of the type of VTR instrumentation within his budget, studying manufacturer's specifications, and, if possible, trying out the equipment himself or working with someone familiar with it who knows how to use it. In some ways, the least expensive non-broadcast VTR equipment is able to accomplish ends in school that more elaborate and expensive VTR instrumentation cannot—and vice versa—depending upon the objectives to which one sets himself in terms of videotape's role in his own special educational situation.

At any rate, take one bit of advice from our communications director: before you send a reel of videotape to someone, clearly mark the make and model number of the instrument which recorded or dubbed it, on the *tape reel* (not on the box). If you receive a reel of unmarked videotape, send it back as quickly as you can. Pretend you did not receive it.

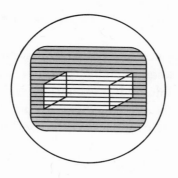

CHAPTER THREE

VIDEOCASSETTES AND EDUCATIONAL TECHNOLOGY

Enthusiasts for the exploitation of videocassette technology and allied systems have called them the "ultimate"
communications instrument for educational and entertainment purposes. A recent magazine advertisement soliciting
funds for investment in a new videocassette production
scheme compares the opportunity it offers the public to
financing Edison's original experiments with light bulbs and
phonographs and/or Marconi's wireless talking machines.
Newsletters and reports on videocassette developments invariably quote one or another technological guru who predicts
that the videocassette holds potentials for school and home
roughly comparable to the invention of indoor plumbing.

Because we have become immune to this glut of
technical hyperbole in which we live, most of us in the field
of education have learned (wisely) to raise an eyebrow
querulously when we are promised—particularly by non-
educators—that they have devised a theory, system or
invention to revolutionize our profession. If we are over
forty, we have lived through countless such revolutions, or

promises of them, nearly all of which have led us back to the same place. We know that change in education, in all its facets, objectives, methods, assumptions and results, does not occur (and has never anywhere occurred) by means of revolution, even in countries where revolutions in political and economic matters have succeeded. Change *does* indeed occur, but it is usually evolutionary, frequently distressingly snailish, often unpredictable, and less the *result* of the intention of revolutionists or reformers than as a *reaction* to changing cultural values, laws and economic factors in society at large that affect not only schools but other institutions also, usually *before* they get to the schoolhouse.

For these very reasons, the hyperbolic assertions of the various videocassette technologists in our midst may, surprisingly, *not* be as wild or irresponsible as they seem at first glance. The perceptive critic of communications technology, keeping his eye on the past, has good reason to believe that winds of change are blowing throughout our entire society. Consider the future of network television, for instance, which may in the next decade go the way of network radio, particularly as today's "wired" cities and communities join cables to produce, inevitably, the first TV-wired nation in the world, offering the home customer dozens of channels of audio and video materials, the possible range of which boggles the mind. Movie-making and exhibition are so different today from twenty-five years ago—and in such bizarre ways—that a clever expert might write an amusing book on the subject; and any man's prediction of what the so-called cinema will become both as a business *and* art form during the next decade is sheer impudence.

Our point is simply that the cultural setting within which videocassette technology will arrive in our schools and homes will inevitably be different, in some measure at least, from the educational and cultural scene that confronts us presently. Technology alone, of course, will not and *cannot* produce this change. Technology never does. Archimedes and his fellow Syracuseans knew enough (and possessed the equipment) to invent a steam engine in the third century B.C. In fact, odds are that one or another of them probably did and subsequently forgot about it. But a steam engine in the Hellenic era was on its face unusable: Who needed a dangerous and delicate machine, particularly in a hot climate, to accomplish expensively the same tasks that slaves could undertake cheaply? What his society wanted from Archimedes was sophisticated military gadgetry and ways and means of distinguishing gold from other metals. And this is what he gave them.

This cultural principle still applies. Our perceptions of technology and invention are colored—even determined—by what we expect technology and invention to accomplish. Like the Hellenes of Archimedes' time, we have an enormous range of *potential* technologies from which we can choose this and that to accomplish the ends we desire. And, by all means, let us flatter ourselves that our range is wider (to our senses) than that of the pre-Christian Greeks. Our choices will, however, be much like theirs, conditioned entirely by what we need—or what we *think* we need—and what we *believe* to be the possible uses of items on the menu of instrumentation before us.

Potential educational applications of videocassette technology will therefore be circumscribed in good measure, of course, by the technical "state of the art," as circumlocutionists say. We will select the instrumentation that works best for our purposes, as well as the kind (eventually standardized, we hope) that accomplishes its ends most economically and conveniently for educators—and at a reasonable profit margin for the industrial machine under whose aegis it falls into our hands. But those other factors—those that prevented Archimedes from inventing the steam engine—must be reckoned with as well. If a dozen or so variables during the next decade somehow fall into place, as they may, the public relations echelon that is currently searching for seed money to finance their revolution in communications may not be the mountebanks they appear to be at first glance. Naturally, the "if" is a large one, but "ifs" are rarely small these days.

What, then, *are* these variables involved in the development of the videocassette and its allied instrumentation into the "ultimate" instrument for educational communications? In other words, what aspects of current educational technology may videocassettes subsume to themselves in function and services, and what new or novel aspects may they present to educators?

Some are fairly obvious but deserve consideration nevertheless, because any or all obvious advantages and disadvantages in the field of technology may be, in the long run, counter-balanced by not-so-obvious counter-disadvantages and counter-advantages that lie latent within them, and in time produce either an insidious or salutary pay-off that nobody expected.

Into the videocassette (whether film, plastic or magnetic tape) may be literally poured everything that currently is stored on reels of motion picture film, be it the film 8mm, Super 8mm, 16mm, 35mm, sound or silent. For better or worse—and here may lie the rub—*all* cassette and cartridge systems will and must, necessarily, convert motion pictures, their colors and their sound tracks, into electronic impulses and produce their *final viewing image on an electronic tube surface.* This surface is, at present, limited to the slightly globular and somewhat distorted TV screens of absolute ubiquity with which we are familiar. True enough, this screen surface, by means of various (now costly) reflection and refraction devices may be *projected* onto a conventional movie screen. But, as those of us who have seen prizefights (and/or *Oh Calcutta!*) on large-screen video projections can testify, a tube is a tube, to paraphrase the late Miss Stein.

At this writing, electronic tube resolution is simply *not* up to the standards of optical projection resolution, in our homes, classrooms or theaters. Seeing a film on TV and later viewing it in a theater usually confirms this. The reason is not easy to pin down, and has nothing whatsoever to do with McLuhanistic nonsense concerning "hot" and "cold" media, because it is a difference that will inevitably be minimized to oblivion *in time*—how much time, we cannot be sure. It relates to the definition of images, screen size, clarity of picture margins, curvature of the viewing surface and, under certain circumstances, differences in social ambience between the TV viewing seance and the audience dynamic of a theater, viewing room and/or classroom.

Reasons for these differences are less important than the fact that *they exist.* And, while the videocassette may one day replace optical film of all kinds (including film cassettes) for all its present uses, it will also necessarily replace the direct optical resolution of photography with electronic resolution of other optical materials as well. In spite of the probability that electronic resolution will some day hold both visual and psychological advantages over conventional motion picture projection (especially when handled by an audio-visual squad in a junior high school with poorly maintained and noisy projectors), electronic resolution must presently be counted as one severe drawback, rarely mentioned, inherent in *all* videocassette systems that qualifies the possibility that videocassettes and cartridges will replace conventional motion pictures in most (but not all) situations. For educators, the difference between optical and electronic resolution may, at times, be critical.

Videocassettes, on the other hand, offer some conveniences that motion picture films cannot duplicate, except when they are housed in cartridges: ease of loading, absence of sprocket holes, small size, complete housing of tape or film, and so forth. These conveniences may, however, be offset by one other present hard fact relating to movies and the way they are used in both schools and universities: It is easier—and requires less skill—to maintain and repair the average 16mm projector than to perform similar functions for the sophisticated electronic and mechanical devices that are used (and contemplated for use) for *all* present and anticipated videocassette systems. And this statement remains true if we compare a motion picture projector merely with the video monitor that displays the cassette image and disregard entirely the entire videocassette playback instrument. Maintenance and repair are major problems in schools of all kinds, and this matter is far from incidental to those of us who must feed and care for educational technology. Educators (and salesmen) know this, but inventors and engineers rarely appear to appreciate fully the firing-line problems of teachers and professors who use film or TV in their classes and the difficulties they encounter in finding technicians with skill enough to maintain and repair their equipment. By and large, 16mm projectors are not difficult to fix and keep in working condition.

Another matter is expense. Will the *entire package* of videocassette instrumentation be as economical as (or more economical than) the present, generally used, 16mm film instrumentation? Even if we knew the realistic costs of one *entire* videocassette system in, say, 1975, many unknown factors would still be involved—that we cannot calculate until the day that competing systems actually meet. At present, 16mm sound projection *seems* cheaper than videocassette projections. New projectors run in the $400-$600 price range, and screens cost about $50 each. Pennies are consumed for maintenance. And film rental charges generally run from $10 (for a dreary "educational" short) to $200 (for a popular or recent film) to print purchases that cost, in general, anywhere from $150 to $1,500 per film.

How will videocassette prices compare to these? Color TV receivers or monitors (only one segment of the system) for classroom use cost from $400 to $600. No price tags have, as of the moment, been fixed to videocassette playback instruments, but a guess that runs between $400 to $1,000 (a pretty wide track) covers the prospective territory. Origination equipment will probably cost about as much as similar reel-to-reel videotape equipment today: that is, from $1,000 up, considering the sophistication involved, whether multiple cameras and lenses, color and other TV razzle-dazzle are involved.

Cassettes for playback only, using film, plastic or discs (like EVR, RCA's projected instrument and Teldec, respectively) will probably be inexpensive to manufacture. Educators will pay most per unit for the *material on them*, that is, their programs. And if they think that videocassette formats will be *one cent* cheaper than film formats of the same program, they misunderstand gravely the free-enterprise system of software distribution.

On the other hand, originating equipment for magnetic tape videocassettes that allows easy plagiarism—to be brutally frank—of open-circuit or cable TV, as well as rented films, may offer to educators bargain-basement deals, despite costs that may run as high as $2,000 for deluxe color recorders and blank cassette prices in the $75 range. The wide use of such devices for the illegal (or non-legal) functions *to which they will inevitably, instantly and widely be put* will occur over the bloodied heads of the producers and owners of the material that is copied and recorded. Note well, however, that (as implied earlier in this book) the practice of audio plagiarism (from discs, reel-to-reel tapes, radio broadcasts and other cassettes and cartridges) is a national pastime that threatens to replace baseball *right now.* And many more than one closed-circuit TV film chain in a school or university has already "taken a projection copy" of a rented feature film on videotape (at about $60 to $100 in tape costs) that is then shown repeatedly in classes for years, instead of re-renting the film. From past experience we learn about the future, and even if copyright legislation eventually clears the miasma that surrounds the proprietary rights of broadcast and rented moving picture and sound materials, the task of enforcing laws that protect legal royalties will be extremely difficult in the degree that bootlegging is made easy and cheap by new technologies like videocassettes.

To boil down the somewhat conjectural comparisons above, 16mm and other types of film projection are unquestionably cheaper, more convenient and superior in resolution to videocassette systems *at present*, as well as more economical. But any judgments made about their future may be similar to comparisons of the Wankel engine of 1975 compared to a V-8 internal combustion engine of 1972. Our guess is that by 1975 conventional film projection and videocassette system manufacturers will have jockeyed themselves into comparable positions in regard to all the above factors, give or take a bit for each.

Costs of total videocassette systems will fall. Picture

fidelity on TV tubes will improve. The problem of repair and maintenance is the stickiest one videocassette entrepreneurs have to face, but it may be beaten by the organization of an echelon of franchised distributors (or renters) of cassette systems who are ready to replace *total* defective components at a moment's notice with working ones and to provide periodical, skilled, effective maintenance. Software prices for videocassettes and films will run neck-and-neck. The variable factor—and one that may upset the entire apple-cart—is the availability, price and potential uses of videocassette equipment for the origination and duplication of what we now call "films." Opportunities to cut film rental and purchase costs in this respect—and they are certain to be extra-legal and annoying opportunities to software producers of *all* kinds— *may* well hurl videocassette instruments (almost certainly those employing oxide tape) into *every* schoolhouse and college in the world that presently shows more than fifty 16mm films a year. This *will* indeed be a revolution, the ramifications of which may echo for years in many unlikely corners of our economy, for many reasons far beyond the purview of this volume.

Will the videocassette reach *beyond* the 16mm projector into the other technologies we find presently in our schools? It well may, once again, *if* educators want it to, or believe that such uses for it are advantageous to their requirements. All videocassette systems will emulate those in prototype at present that permit "stop-frame" techniques in order to hold still pictures (or "single-frames") on a TV tube for as long as the viewer desires. Filmstrips and slides will therefore be able to be programmed into cassettes of every type, with or without narration. Once again, film and plastic cassettes or cartridges will have to be manufactured by software companies. *Magnetic videotape cassettes will permit home-brewing.*

Cassettes here will offer two advantages over the kind of still-picture devices presently in use in most schools. First, it will probably be possible to store a tremendous number of still pictures and graphic material on a single cassette, particularly if sound narration (which eliminates the "stop-frame" potential) does *not* accompany it, or is provided by a synchronized audiotape. Counting index instruments, which indicate the exact number of inches of film or tape unrolled in each cassette, will allow one easily to locate specific single-frame material on each cassette. (One single film or tape videocassette may well, in theory, be able to store the entire film strip *and* slide library in full color of a good-sized school or college.) Second, the fuss and bother of arranging slide shows, the unhappy burden of many art teachers and others, will not entirely be eliminated. But a complete program may be organized at the instructor's leisure and fed into a cassette well in advance of its presentation, eliminating thereby hazards of defective slide-feeders, both human and mechanical.

At another end of the spectrum of electronic sophistication, videocassettes may replace (or, when needed, add moving pictorial supplements to) every sort of voice retrieval system presently in use in schools, colleges and professional schools. By this we mean language laboratories, dial access systems, computer-assisted instruction and other types and variations of educational technology, dispensed both to groups in classes and individuals in listening (and viewing) carrels. Flexible utilization of moving pictures and sound combined with other educational tools has been, until now, largely the province of education visionaries who dream up "schools of tomorrow," efforts that often are grounded not in the thoughtful consideration of the contextual processes of learning in its many phases and moods but in simple-minded attempts to relate atomized behavior objectives (or pay-offs) to available technology. On the surface these pseudo-prophets make sense, but in practice they usually fail even according to their own limited criteria of success.

Most grandiose dreams that radically reorganize present schooling on all levels into the matrix of a panoply of gadgets (and competing notions of how to use them) are almost invariably nonsensical and non-productive—except for the cash flow they release from giant foundations into the pockets of those affable dreamers who think them up. Video dial access systems, computerized instruction and individual programs for skill training may indeed one day utilize videocassettes, just as their prototypes today utilize reel-to-reel sound tape and audiocassettes. But this Topsy will not be born full-blown. Videocassette facilities will and must be introduced slowly and thoughtfully into present technologically oriented educational systems, most of which still require continual modifications and revision before they will eventually work as well as older methods or meet their own educational objectives.

Videocassettes used on a grand scale—in the manner of today's more ambitious information retrieval systems—will undoubtedly require both sophisticated and extremely expensive technological gear, as well as an echelon of full-time, expertly trained service personnel in every installation to keep them working properly.

One responsible prediction is therefore in order here: If and when such systems are constructed and used, picture output will unquestionably originate from one or another of the videocassette instruments that will be available at the time—*not* from film chains, motion picture projectors or reel-to-reel videotape playback instruments. Whether the software they employ will depend upon film, plastic or electronic tape is another matter, contingent entirely upon factors already discussed. But pictorial material of all kinds will be fed into these systems, even the most modest, entirely by means of videocassettes, *simply because no other form of picture origination available by then will, in all probability, lend itself to the automation that information retrieval systems require.*

Videocassettes will be ideal for these systems, should they eventuate, despite the fact that present, elaborate installations seem presently to work well with reel-to-reel *sound* tape and even phonograph records. Sound recording and picture recording are different beasts one from the other—and so, incidentally, is the manner and condition of their reception. A carrel or booth satisfactory for listening purposes by means of a speaker or headphones may or *may not* be satisfactory for viewing a moving image in color. While some experiments have indicated rough specifications for televising in schools,* similar guidelines have not yet been clearly delineated for viewing TV monitors under the kinds of circumstances that programmed instruction, information retrieval systems and study laboratories create for both students and teachers. And such specifications will be needed—probably worked out by trial-and-error in good time—before videocassettes will effectively be integrated into old systems or built into new ones.

Unlike money, Gresham's law does not necessarily apply to educational technology. The new does not always, or even often, drive out the old. Chalk boards are infinitely superior to overhead projectors—for certain purposes. Slides are better than films for others. Textbooks perform functions that the

---

*See George N. Gordon, *Classroom Television*, pp. 190-197.

most sophisticated CAI systems presently in operation may well find impossible to accomplish. And, if a pun is forgiven, we all know the old saw about Mark Hopkins and the log. Despite prognostications to the contrary made a decade or two ago, instructional TV has *not* had much of an impact on American schooling—except in military and other training programs that may hardly be dignified by the term "education." Nor has it, to date, displaced or limited the use of former educational technologies, even the most primitive, to any substantial degree.

Crude minds prefer to think of all technological devices as necessarily replacing or sending into oblivion *something*. And the crudeness is justified when we consider, outside the world of education, what air travel has done (or we have allowed it to do) to railroad and ship passenger transport. The automobile *did* indeed replace the horse, on our streets—but not on our racetracks, where they now co-exist as contestants in games. But the world of education is not a crude place—although many crude minds are presently tinkering with its destiny. Videocassettes will find their proper places in our schools, neither as swiftly nor as sweepingly as contemporary prophets of the moment antici-pate, but side-by-side with other, older technologies (some of them simple but effective) that have served education long and well. The exact configurations of this mix will be written by teachers (not manufacturers of hard- or software) from successes and failures in the crucible of their own and our experiences, either using prefabricated software (as films do today) or opening up for educators an entirely new and easily accomplished world of locally originated materials coordi-nated to other educational technologies, old and new.

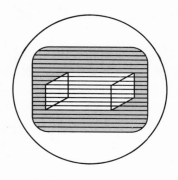

CHAPTER FOUR

VIDEOCASSETTES AND THE NEW MEDIA CENTERS

One persistent dream of American education—beatific for some and nightmarish for others—is the crude but impressive-sounding notion that whatever it is that the technological revolution of the past century or so has done for our nation's lifestyle and standards of living, eating and playing, it will also do for its standards of schooling. Since the publication of Dewey's *School and Society* at the turn of the century, the never-ending call from a wide segment of the educational community has been for our educators to "catch up" with the rest of society's consumption and use of technology.

Strangely, in the authors' opinion, nobody has yet provided many good reasons *why* this supposed culture-lag, as it is often called, *should* be closed up, except more or less naively to note that technology seems to operate very well in matters of transportation, food distribution and mass entertainment; and that education, being in some persons' view a similar commodity, must profit similarly from technology.

Arguments by analogy are dangerous, and, in the light

of a current vogue of discontents with the so-called side-effects and fallout from all of our technology at large, this one becomes unsettlingly perilous when carried to its extremes. Hence, its antithesis: the blatant rejection of the analogous, one-to-one equation of schooling with other aspects of culture—even mass entertainment (for good reasons)—and the immense skepticism that has, in effect, not only preserved this culture-lag to the present moment, but interprets it as a virtue. Mass technology is not just a benign deity, the argument runs, and its relevance to many human activities, from the appreciation of poetry to boxing to sustaining interpersonal relationships, is at best tangential, facilitative and often expendable.

Prophets are not necessarily accurate in their warnings, but most of our major seers in the recent past (and those looking into entrails at present) seem, with Huxley and Orwell in the lead, to be more concerned about the *over*-application, *over*-use and *mis*-use of *all* technology (and "know-how") than about its *under*-application—the basic complaint of most present educational technologists. Because he is much a man-of-the-moment (or the recent past) and reflects so cleverly the "progressive" notions of the average man, Arthur C. Clarke (among others) has captured this concern strikingly both in the book and film *2001, A Space Odyssey,* by articulating the man-in-the-street's present concerns *ad absurdum.* He therefore provides us with a clear vision of our present fears in raw form. In much the same manner, of course, the works of Jules Verne still offer us an accurate picture of the Victorian mind by examining, nearly a century ago, European attitudes toward technology as they were felt by many thinking people *then.*

In this present volume, we have tried to steer a sane course between what we believe are attractive extremes, both of which contain much of value, but both of which are indeed being carried too far by many educators who, by and large, are far less imaginative than novelists, and who manage somehow to justify blatantly *both* the fears and frustrations of their detractors.

In the first place, educational technology is simply *not*, either entirely or in great part, analogous to other types of technology. And those who center their projections into the future upon this mistaken assumption have been childishly misled. Many, many educators have swallowed this analogy hook and bait whole, and are now living to regret it. It will be as true tomorrow, naturally, of videocassette technology applied to education compared to technology used for purposes of entertainment as it is, at present, for any other mass instrument of communication, be it TV, film or audiotape.

In the second place, while much modern technology remains quite irrelevant to contemporary schooling of many sorts, it has already demonstrated its ancillary utility to the total institution of education in our culture in many dramatic ways, starting, possibly, with the humble school bus (that has made possible an entirely new type of high school, as we shall see) to the sophisticated instrumentation that offers medical students a programmed, computerized robot "patient" upon whom they may test their healing techniques without worrying about his mortality. To deny the utility of what already operates effectively is not only quixotic, it is worse than hook-swallowing, because it is inexcusably dim-witted.

While the following statement may certainly discourage both enthusiasts and detractors of contemporary technology in schooling (leaving, we hope, a sufficient number of readers to continue further into this book), the major role of technology in education is, we believe, *facilitative rather than innovative or creative.* And we base this modest but far from axiomatic observation not upon a dream of a future society that may never come to be, but upon the history of when, where and how technology has, in the past, succeeded, and even thrived, in American schools during the past half-century.

At this point, it would be simple to wax widely (and irresponsibly) about media centers, libraries and computerized access systems of today and tomorrow, all of them utilizing videocassettes, making available to teachers and students from kindergartens to research seminars "the vast heritage of Western Man," as the cliché goes. Constructing stainless steel and glass Utopias on paper is both a revoltingly simple and a widely practiced sport among educators, nearly as popular as "reforming" education, the weariest and most tiresome gambit played by members of the academic community and its hangers-on.

What, first, let us ask, may media centers and libraries realistically look forward to regarding the use or distribution of videocassettes?

Before any other considerations, we must note that concepts of media centers as discrete and different from libraries are everywhere breaking down, largely, at the moment, at the behest of financial imperatives, and in spite of the protests of older audio-visual types who maintain the view that librarians, working as they do largely with books and magazines, are not privy to cabals involved in utilizing film projectors, slides and tape recorders. Some of their complaints are well taken: American librarians are, by and large, notoriously clannish and stuffy, in and outside of schools, pathologically averse to talking above a whisper and psychotic adversaries of cigarette smoking (in this latter matter, the British are far more civilized) who frequently equate the effectiveness of a library with how *little* its carefully catalogued books are opened, read, circulated, underlined or otherwise dirtied by use. A good number seem to regard reading in anything but a silent, upright sitting position as a vice, and many of our nation's best scholars will go to any strategem to stay out of libraries, obtaining their information, by hook or crook, from other sources.

Mainly because of new pressures upon it, the contemporary school and/or community library simply *cannot* continue as the cozy repository of re-bound books and neat reading rooms that it has been for the past century. More and more of the material it dispenses will be placed on diminutive film of one sort or another: ergo, the need for projectors, reading machines, etc. Xerography and other types of copy-work are fast intruding into old routines. Planners for new libraries must face the fact that ever-increasing amounts of data are now being recorded in sound on tapes and discs and that motion pictures (whether on film or videotape) constitute today a far larger repository of primary data (and are therefore of scholarly interest) than *all the books that were ever published in the United States* did in, say, 1920. This also means that the introduction into even modest-sized libraries of access systems of various degrees of sophistication to retrieve this glut of materials and keep it in order is inevitable.

Moans and groans by audio-visualists, therefore, that they are losing hegemony over "non-print media," as they call recordings and movies, are somewhat sad in the light of their now-ancient functions as hard- and software keepers (and the opprobrium they have often received because of it). But the movement of media centers into, and finally their amalgamation with, libraries as we know them is, nevertheless, as inevitable as the rising of the moon. The old-time AV custodians may take a measure of consolation in the discontents that librarians feel as their neat, Morocco-bound world disintegrates in front of their eyes, happy in the knowledge that tomorrow's library (and its many diversions) brings as little cheer to the librarian's heart as it does to that of the media specialist. But come the day must—and will—and, for this reason, peace treaties are presently being negotiated (in whispers, one assumes) between audio-visualists and librarians, the combatants in this meaningless battle on—almost—a world-wide scale, signifying nothing.

At this point in their development, it is almost certain that cassettes or cartridges will become the main standard instruments for the "read-out," projection or for playing of both audio and visual materials in tomorrow's library. Master copies (from which cassettes are dubbed) may be stored on audio- or videotape reels, as well as on cellulose film reels, to insure that both full sound and picture fidelity is preserved permanently in its original form. Problems of storage are enormous in this regard, of course, and it is unlikely that most small high school or elementary school libraries will require or be able to house a wide stock of such masters. In these institutions, finished and complete cartridges or cassettes will probably be ordered, more or less as needed, from centrally located duplication centers that will also maintain complex and varied instrumentation to produce cassette and cartridge formats as required by libraries, schools and universities.

What sort of technology will these cartridges or cassettes employ? Here our crystal ball clouds a bit, but certain parameters of reasonableness, may, at the moment, be drawn. Using new high-fidelity chromium dioxide tape when necessary (and the Dolby noise-reduction process, an ingenious electronic method of eliminating "tape hiss" in audio recording), the small two-reel audiocassette will probably become the standard library instrument for sound playback, even for stereophonic musical recordings of high quality. Students will either listen to cassette tapes in library carrels or take them home for use on their own playback instruments (or both), returning them to the library either for redistribution or re-recording.

As far as visual materials are concerned—and here we are referring largely to what are today known as "films"—libraries will deal in two *types*, or at least two different *classes*, of materials, and the instrumentation chosen to meet these needs will necessarily be determined in some measure by the category into which they fall.

On one hand, libraries will be called upon to distribute *permanent* motion picture materials (*The Birth of a Nation* is an example as is, possibly, a newsreel of President Kennedy's inauguration ceremony) in a cassette or cartridge format that may quickly and easily be projected, most probably on a TV tube, but possibly, also, optically. If it may be circulated beyond the library for home use, so much the better.

On the other hand, *transitory* materials (dubs from cable TV, commercial and public video, locally originated video lessons, movies rented for one-shot showings, etc.) will also have to be distributed and, to some degree, screened or projected in libraries by library personnel as well. There will be little need to keep such cassettes or cartridges beyond their immediate period of use, and they will therefore either be re-recorded with new transitory materials (if they employ magnetic tape) or discarded (if they employ an inexpensive enough film or plastic process).

At present, the only videocassette or cartridge systems that meet *both* of these requirements are those that employ *magnetic videotape*. But, as the technology of videocassettes evolves, it may be neither desirable nor necessary to utilize any *single* system or type of instrumentation for both permanent and transitory purposes. Nor is there any inevitably predetermined reason why oxide tape is better for cassette or cartridge use than cellulose or plastic (as in the now-dormant EVR, film cartridge projectors and disc instruments) except that, at the present moment, *only* magnetic tape has a potential for *local originating capacity.* That is, the processing of film or plastic is complicated and requires highly specialized equipment and techniques, whereas the ability to record material on videotape cassettes is potentially relatively simple, probably within the financial reach and competences of the staff of even an elementary school library—although *no* such originating instruments are, at this writing, earmarked for the general educational market within the near future.

Regardless of the threat they portend to manufacturers of playback instruments using film and plastic (such as EVR and videodisc devices), no-nonsense announcements by American and foreign firms of the potential availability of equipment for magnetic tape videocassette *recording,* its approximate price range and the date it will become available to the public are doing much, at this point, to stabilize the unresolved status of the videocassette as a variety of library—and educational—software. Because so many technical and educational possibilities loom for different and incompatible videocassette playback instruments—including those being developed by Eastman Kodak and others—that employ old, familiar Super 8mm movie film that is eventually "projected" onto a TV tube, it is the *needs* of educators, and librarians particularly, that will eventually determine the specific types of equipment which, in the long run, will be developed, marketed, standardized and used—and will survive the cut-throat competition to come.

Manufacturers of most of this equipment seem to calculate their commercial future in exactly the opposite fashion, assuming that their customers will find applications for any and all types of hardware they produce. Looking at the world as businessmen (a perfectly respectable perspective) they simply do not *know* librarians or understand educators or how they think and work—nor are they really familiar with their professional motives. The resolution of the present problems concerning the incompatibilities of various systems will *not* be solved by collusions of commercial interests creating standardizations of hardware that result in offering to schools and libraries *one* or *two* types of videocassette instrument and saying, in effect, "Take 'em or leave 'em." If this instrumentation does not contain features that librarians and educators feel they will find useful and that they require in their institutions *as they want to run them*—and originating or copying capacities *may be* the critical element here—they will most certainly "leave 'em," as they have left many other types of educational gadgetry that have come down the pike in the past twenty-five years. (Remember those fancy multi-media machines for administering and scoring multiple-choice tests on the spot?)

Standardization of videocassettes, perhaps into two or three basic systems, each performing *one* function most easily and cheaply, will therefore never be achieved by the expedient of meetings and conferences of manufacturers or inventors, but rather as the result of considering closely *the needs of the people who will utilize them,* particularly librarians and media specialists, in the references of this present chapter. Unless such an inventory of applications guides the hands of *both* videocassette software and hardware entrepreneurs servicing the educational world, they are best advised to concentrate their talents upon the home entertainment market where, as song and story have it, consumer needs may be created from dust by means of advertising and exploitation. Not so in our schools, ladies and gentlemen—particularly in libraries. *Not so at all!*

Flying a little higher and wider now, there is no reason why videocassette technology may not also be married to present instruments of dial access and computerized and/or programmed instruction, most of it still on the drawing board, but some actually in use. The authors' prejudices and experience lead them to believe that automated education of this type is most useful in *training* (skill training, particularly) and for indoctrination, particularly of the kind offered by large corporations to new or re-assigned employees. In such instructional situations, motivation is high and the age and status of the students lead them to center their interest not on beating the educational game, but on actually understanding concepts, developing skills and comprehending their roles and relationships of their jobs to an entire organization.

Automated education—even utilizing simple linear or branching programmed systems that employ books or paper and pencil gadgets—does indeed, it has been proven, lead both student and teacher towards achieving terminal *behavioral* objectives, in Skinner's, Mager's and other behaviorists' odd construction of the term "objectives." But they do not, usually, head out towards education in Whitehead's, Dewey's or Mumford's construction of the word. In fact, they run in quite the opposite direction much of the time in practice, and invariably in theory. But their use in schooling—or in some of the types of activities that occur today in our schools—is both obvious and beyond dispute. As these tools become increasingly sophisticated, that is, as they depend more and more upon programmed, computerized "memories" to jockey students through their metaphorical mazes, games and gambits, they are likely to turn up far more widely than at present in high school and university courses of study dominated by the art of skill building—language study being one major, notable and important example.

If we remain with this latter, rather clear-cut aspect of the contemporary curriculum, it is obvious how and to what degree the introduction of the videocassette's capacity for using pictures adds still another dimension to the widespread and effective use of audiotapes in teaching languages in a language laboratory. At present, if a student at a station or carrel in such a lab wishes to relate the conversational lesson in French that he is studying by means of an audiotape to the printed text of it (whether or not he may answer back or repeat on a separate sound track the voice he hears), he must follow some sort of printed or written materials as he listens. This procedure sounds simple to accomplish, but a short tour of language labs as used in various institutions proves otherwise. Possibly some esoteric variation of Murphy's Law* operates in these installations, but the problem of coordinating the right text material with the right audio material is often both apparently grave and beyond human solution. Videocassettes might run *both* a sight track (letters of a sentence passing at reading speed before the student's eyes) and carry a coordinated sound track for a student, varying, perhaps, the use of each for testing or response purposes.

Starting with the language laboratory, it is possible now to glean how varied coordinations of visual with audio and print material may be accomplished in almost all self-directed

---

*An old Army saying, "If anything can go wrong, it will," usually applied to technology and systems.

instructional programs, whether or not they follow our present notions of programmed instruction, and regardless of their sophistication by means of computer gadgetry. Of course, video stimuli have already been widely used in this type of instruction by means of printed materials like pictures and maps, slides, motion pictures in rear-screen boxes, and even by means of videotape transmitted over a film chain and fed by cable into student carrels. But in most of the former instances, they have hardly been worth the time and trouble it takes first to set them up, and second, to keep them operating properly, particularly if they are subjected to heavy wear.

Videocassette technology will override these inevitable "bugs," if the cassettes and allied instruments operate at about the same level of efficiency that sound cassettes and cartridges do today. And there is no *technical* reason why they should not, especially if their engineers resist the urge (to which they gave in for some audio technology) to miniaturize the *mechanical* aspects of their devices beyond both reason and utility. Schools which employ videocassettes in programmed and computerized instruction will require rugged, simple-to-operate and easily repaired instrumentation as well as trouble-free cassettes, somewhat peculiar specifications to request of a technology that is intrinsically delicate, sophisticated and extremely complex. Instruments of this sort, however, are today available among the wide variety of videorecorders on the market, and they are *not necessarily* found among the most highly-touted lines of prestigious manufacturers, American, European and Japanese. Such specifications are obviously not impossible for videocassette engineers to achieve. But they must first recognize the priority of needs of the people who will use their wares— needs that educators will gladly, we think, pay premium prices to meet.

Coordinating videocassette facilities with programmed and computerized instruction (and, for that matter, with systems of dial access and instant retrieval of audio and video information) is too amorphous and hazy a topic to discuss in detail at present, first, because it is difficult for one to pin-point the major uses for these educational innovations in the near, to say nothing of the remote, future. Major technological innovations of this sort in instruction have not, to date, traveled far beyond local utilization here and there: a college in Montana, a high school in Alabama, etc.—where they invariably work well, mostly because the people responsible for thinking them up have made it impossible for them to fail. And most visiting "experts" and "critics" know this and therefore hesitate to endorse their wider use. Second, we are still uncertain and of many minds about videocassettes themselves in regard to critical matters like costs, ease of operation, durability and, possibly the major issue in their use, the nature of picture and sound resolution that they permit. This last matter will be critical in determining attitudes both of teachers and students towards the systems and programs into which they are integrated, although it is blithely assumed at present that a moving picture optically projected on a screen, a rear screen and/or resolved into lines on an electronic tube, or projected onto a screen from that tube, are all, from the consumer's view-point, the same.

Granting not one jot of his peculiar mysticism to Dr. McLuhan, they are *not* all equal in quality and psychological impact *at the moment* simply because of the basic differences in the hardware and software they employ, rather than Canadian inherent "cross-media" voodoo. These differences can be—and will be—ironed out, but at present they remain matters of some concern to those who are considering and planning potential educational uses for videocassettes.

In sum, and to return to the observations that began this chapter, educators have been, and are, and probably always will be, ready and competent to use in our schools whatever in modern (for them) technology they think is relevant to their functions as educators. Note well, however, that they have never, at least in North America, been inclined to amalgamate *any* type of new technology into their arts and sciences of teaching simply because, like Everest, it is *there*. In this conservatism, we esteem them wise and prudent. It probably explains, in great measure, many of the successes of American education, although it is relevant also to its notable and egregious failures.

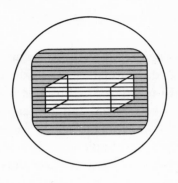

CHAPTER FIVE

VIDEOCASSETTES AND INFORMAL EDUCATION

Once upon a time, securely ensconced in the labyrinthian byways of historical anonymity, there lived a king who faced a serious dilemma with his people. His was an agricultural kingdom, slowly emerging from a frustrating nomadic life, whose welfare was dependent upon an annual wheat crop yield.

Of course, the crop this year was fruitful, but something went awry. When one ate the bread that was made from the wheat, it unfortunately made one mad. The king was now apprehensive, for to allow the people to partake from the granaries would madden the populace and destroy the kingdom. To forbid them to eat would produce certain famine.

The wise men of the kingdom were hurriedly called into conference. And the wisdom flowed loud and long, and the theses and hypotheses were examined and re-examined for all their respective nuances and implications for the future welfare of the kingdom. A consensus finally emerged, and the king decreed that the people were to eat of the wheat and suffer the madness rather than the ravages of famine. However, there were those to be chosen from among the people as a special class whose chief role was to remind the people that they were indeed mad. And those chosen were heroes and villains at one and the same time. For the people turned upon them and insisted that it was *they* who were mad. At times these "stabilizers" of society were considered prophets, priests, ministers and rabbis; at other times, they were wizards, alchemists and Merlins; at times they were cabinet members, princes and feudal lords; at other times they were poets, musicians and artists; at times they were pedants, scholars and teachers.

And what were some of the madnesses they told to the people? These were some: in a world where the "great" religions and the not-so-"great" religions preach brotherly love, killing and war and threats of war remained rampant. And so the prophets, priests, ministers and rabbis were often martyred and vilified, laughed at and ignored. In a world where science and knowledge could free the world of superstition and fear from the whimsies of gods, witches, devils and nether-world fantasies, intellectual and physical slavery still existed, prescribed by institutionalized author-ities and sanctioned by many state entities. And so the chemist became the alchemist and the astronomer became the astrologer and a host of Galileos, ancient and modern, were proscribed. In a world where the dignity of man and his innate right for self-fulfillment and freedom of expression became a realizable ideal, man everywhere was reduced to a manipulable entity for the betterment of institutionalized entities other than himself—and so injustice ran rampant, equality evanesced into inaccessible recesses and individual dignity was encrusted with myriad indignities. And the cabinet ministers and lords and princes were Machiavellian in

intent. In a world where the awesome beauties of nature and
its obsessive multifarious moods and forms and tones and
textures and processes are hauntingly awe-inspiring, the
creative artists were proscribed from their celebrations, for
the state thought them unsettling influences, and what did
filter out to the people from them often were insipid
palliatives of unimaginative and authoritarian dictates to
convince the masses that their state of madness was the
norm.

And so Plato even took away their citizenship. And then
there was a class who, in reminding the people of their
madness, were forced to taste the cup of hemlock like
Socrates. The people, in their madness, even charged the
teachers with poisoning the minds of their children. And, in
order to avoid the wrath of the mad populace, the teachers
tried Socratic dialogues, and they failed. They tried scholasti-
cism, and they failed. They tried the lecture, the seminar, and
with the help of the Chinese and the advent of printing, they
tried the book as a replacement for the scrolls, and they
failed. They tried professional and vocational education,
prescribed and elective liberating arts and liberating sciences,
and they failed. They tried rote and not-so-rote methods, and
they failed. They tried co-educational and non-co-educational
education, and they failed. They tried progressive education
and the concept of the school as an embryonic community as
the philosophy of their education, and they failed. They tried
the segregated and the integrated school, the neighborhood
school and the bussed school, the public and the private
school, and they failed. They tried the school enriched with,
or totally addicted to, the television, the film, the radio
technologies as supplements to, or at times replacements for,
the books, the teachers, the lectures, the seminars, the
workshops, the demonstrations, and they failed. They tried

the closed school and the open school, and they failed.

They tried the formal school and then the informal school, and they got confusing answers, because, in their madness, they began to ask themselves a mad question, namely, "What is failure? If we *re-define the term,* possibly we can succeed!" And so, in the land of the mad, the question remained: will the informal one "succeed" where all the others have not? If the question does not seem to answer itself for the reader, then it seems the reader has lost the lessons of history. For in the ever-changing needs and in the shifting relationships within the fabric of society, *no* state and *no* institution has been able to stabilize a perspective on the rampant madness of the people or define for certain who *is*, in fact, sane or mad.

If, as the old adage goes, the child is father to the man, then perhaps in the training and education of the child lies a promise for the future of man. This is the common wisdom of our presently "mad" society. Whenever social ills or communal psychopathy are discussed, education is invariably the panacea that will solve all problems, at least according to people who are not educators themselves. Therefore, they gladly turn the task of ultimate redemption to teachers, professors and administrators, most of whom are ill prepared for the weighty burdens society thrusts at them.

Our culture expects enormous results from its educators and puts a greater percentage of its national wealth into their hands to achieve them than any other country in the world. However, we must always be wary of rising expectations. For as promising as they are, *unfulfilled* they are the crucible of further frustration and increased madness. With each new philosophic concept in education, with each innovation in educational technology, we have seen promises that have boomeranged into increased despair. The stretches of our educational horizons often seem despairing. And where it was said of Eleanor Roosevelt by Adlai Stevenson that she "would rather light a candle than curse the darkness," our generation is bent on cursing the darkness, because we have grown suspicious of candles and aware that they do not produce much illumination and constitute enormous fire hazards.

And what latest panacea do we have in education for affecting benignly this adverse set of circumstances? From England, from parts of the European continent, from intellectual oases in America has come an anti-formalistic philosophy of education which in seeking to minimize the authority of the teacher as a presenter has been labelled "Informal Education," "Open Classroom Education," "Corridor Education" and other epithets. Charles E. Silberman, in his book *Crisis in the Classroom,* sees this as an individualized experience-oriented education. Originally devised for British Infant Schools, its philosophy (or methodology) has gained a foothold on the continent and in the U.S.A. The "open" part of this education refers to the breaking down of traditional classroom space, the fracturing of old-fashioned curricula and the dispensing with time blocks and age groupings in formal education. Each child supposedly advances according to his own interests and at his own pace. The environment, "open" as it may seem, is nevertheless inevitably patterned and guided by the teacher. Skills and concepts are learned in an integrated manner through activity, with enjoyment of varied materials. The role of the teacher is as much affected as is the behavior of the child.

If, as Piaget says, thought is internalized action, then Dewey's learning-by-doing is a corollary concept in trying to develop the unique skills and thoughts of each child at his own rate and in his own way and in the distinctive manner of

the environment from which he comes. In the open classroom, interest centers are set up—in place of rows of desks
facing the teacher. At each interest center, the children work
and play with continuing projects in a workshop atmosphere.
Conceivably, there can be a book center, a math center, a
woodworking center, a television center and so forth. The
children whose interest span changes constantly can move
from one interest center in the class to another, almost at
will, without preconceived time-spans, bells, curriculum goals
and structures to follow.

This type of "family grouping," as it is sometimes
called, precludes the lecture role of the teacher as authority
and eliminates the rote method of learning and responding.
Where pleasing the teachers to achieve a good grade was a
goal for the student in formal education, expressing himself
in his own way with his own time-space resources in a family
grouping is a key element in informal education. The need
for the student to adjust to the teacher becomes minimal.

*The videocassette may be a most viable tool for this
setting.* Because the atmosphere is relaxed, stimulation for
innovation is not throttled by an anxiety over failure or low
grades. Pleasing the teacher becomes a secondary goal to that
of externalizing thought by creative action. Since television is
ubiquitous in American homes and is part of the infant
experience and on-going experience beyond the infancy
practically to the grave, the use of this instrument in a
creative way in the classroom is a natural extension of the
student's home environment to the informal environment of
the open classroom. Starting in a comfortable way with as
familiar a home-object as the television set, children moving
freely from interest center to interest center around the open
classroom will find familiar comfort at the television center.

To the very youngest, the teacher may distribute

videotape cassettes that relate to the reading, writing and mathematical skills that each child has come to perceive and utilize in the other interest centers. Manufacturers will have to be careful technologically to design their videocassettes so that the least mechanical-minded and the least dexterous of normal children in the lower grades can *load and play and replay the cassettes at will.* In this way, the bright and the not-so-bright, the normal and the slow child may supplement, enrich and stimulate his learning at his own characteristic pace. The developing of serializing skills and conceptual learning in an interrelated way, concerned with the child as an individual, is what is achieved here. The cassette can instruct, direct and guide, and it may correct and direct the learning experience in such a way as to create the resourceful child instead of the disciplined and frightened one. In an integrated way, the child may conceive and solve problems for himself and carry on his own research to do so, even on the level of the earliest grades.

On the more advanced levels of the grade school, and in the junior high school and the senior high school, students are able to use the cassette with even more sophistication. A class in current events might be given a portable tape recorder with a single camera and zoom lens in 1/4 inch, 1/2 inch or 1 inch videotape modes and visit the local newspaper for the recording of interviews with editors and reporters on a given subject of current interest to the school community. This tape cassette may then be duplicated and/or played not only for the open classroom students who completed the assignments, but may also be circulated among interested classrooms throughout the entire school.

Here is a highly resourceful use of the cassette. And it need not be very expensive if costs are amortized and cassettes are reused by wiping and recording over them. A tape library may also be built up of current topics to lend a sense of historical sweep and continuity with the past without too much expense. Thus, rather than contorting the student to fit into a prescribed curriculum, the curriculum may grow out of the interests and needs of the students. The role of the teacher in supervising those interests becomes one in which he or she creates more meaningful relationships with all the other areas of learning. The academic skills of reading, writing and mathematics come into *all* activity and hence are not taught in isolation.

In the formal classroom, where the student learned how to "do" the multiplication table, it was done with that as an end in itself. In the informal class, it *ideally* becomes a method in solving a problem. The best kind of learning is experienced learning, and the videocassette, both in playback and in the making, can be a most effective experience. However, manufacturers would be wise to see to it that some form of standardization is achieved in order to assure the interchangeability among classes and schools of video-cassettes. As difficult as the cooperation among them may be to achieve, with each striking out with his own format, videocassettes will either be standardized by conquest or cooperation. If by conquest, the battle will be long and bloody. If by cooperation, educators will find cassettes at their fingertips in less than a decade.

We are here referring to, and base our examples upon, not only videocassettes which contain prefabricated software (most useful in informal education for young children) but also videocassettes which permit *origination* and *duplication* of learning material at the school and classroom level. This means that we have eliminated from our consideration cassette formats that are merely convenient projection devices utilizing either film or plastic tapes or discs, that we believe have *only limited application in informal schools.* At present, only the magnetic tape videocassette offers the *potential* for origination, but technology may present new options in the future. And all manufacturers have been disarmingly quiet about this critical facet of cassette technology. At the present writing, there exist pitifully few prototypes of any kind of cassette origination system for us to examine closely and experiment with (except very complicated ones), and the first manufacturers to bring them at a reasonable price to a hungry market are likely to dictate standards for the entire videocassette industry for a generation to come.

If the teacher's role may *seem* somewhat changed or demeaned by the independent use of videocassettes by students, in reality it is not. Whereas he or she formerly was an ultimate source of information, preparing lesson plans and delivering them to a whole class or series of classes, the teacher now guides and leads the child or child-groups into ways of solving problems in order to develop in them a knack for independent thinking. The teacher then becomes a resource person who, in consultation with the students, directs the utilization of everything within the classroom environment. If the videocassette is to be a part of that environment, it had best be *easy and simple for him or her to use.* The specific idea of development for the week approximates the previously prescribed curriculum units in formalized education. Thus, crucial to the use of the videocassette in the open classroom is the teacher's ability continually to direct and redirect interest and activity.

By observing the student, the teacher determines the needs of the child. This requires a good deal of sophistication on the part of the teacher. Having ascertained the need, the teacher then directs the activity in exploratory fashion until the need is satisfied in a way which coincides with the developmental growth of the student. Ascertaining the growth of the student and recording his progress is a matter based on astute observations by the teacher rather than on the results of formalized tests and grade results. The role of the teacher as disciplinarian and information-dispenser has faded away; the role is now one of consultant and guidance director in a classroom environment whose ceremonial setting more resembles the home than the throne room.

As one can see immediately, informal education turns its back almost entirely on the trappings of educational innovation usually associated with technology: articulated, precise behavioral objectives; fine, quantitative measures of achievement; programmed sequences of learning and both systems and "systems theory." Not only is informal education indifferent to the basic assumptions of so-called "human engineering," it is downright antagonistic towards them, regarding them, in fact, as *anti-educational*. This stance will prove to be the single most significant factor either in the triumph of informal schooling or its downfall. And it is simply too soon for the objective observer to predict reliably how the wind will blow. Most important, a middle-road compromise between informal education and systematic education is, in our opinion, impossible. Technology, however—and we believe particularly the videocassette—may be a bridge between them, because it can be useful in many ways to accomplish the ends of both.

Espousers of the open classroom are careful to point out that the "open" is not synonymous with "free," "unstructured" or whimsically characterized random student activity and accidental learning. They are careful to distinguish between the mistakes of Dewey-ish progressivists of yesterday and their own anti-authoritarian, multi-interest, environmental classroom. Informalists point out that, in their opinion, our present educational methods and philosophies are simply not adequate to the present and anticipated needs of the future school population.

Most informalists will point out that it is not behavior problems that produce the failure to learn. On the contrary, they say, it is the children's failure to learn that produces behavior problems. Perhaps even more important than the school, as influences in the learning of the child, are the home, the neighborhood and the peer groups from which the child comes. The above set parameters to achievement and socio-economic mobility for the child in society. Of considerably less importance, they argue, is class size, teaching methodology, school size, lecture versus seminar, groupings and other ancient academic concepts in the catalyzing of learning.

There are those among both the informalists and formalists who still regard all educational technology as less important than its manufacturers and salesmen tout it to be. After all, another storage and retrieval audio-visual system, cheap to install, easy to operate and flexible to use does not seem the panacea to all, or most, educational problems. Teachers often have an aversion to educational technology in that it tends, as they see it, to dehumanize education. Here, then, the role of the *teacher* in the utilization of technology becomes most important. If the teacher recedes into the background of the learning process and abdicates his or her active role as a consultative resource person who interlaces the use of technology with purposive direction, then the dehumanization process will readily occur.

On the other hand, the videocassette transcends the limiting factors of space and time in classroom learning.

The videocassette *may* be used to overcome the shortage

of specialized, skilled teaching experts, to stimulate curriculum innovations and to assist in the open classroom concept by helping to establish an anti-authoritarian, relaxed classroom atmosphere. The cassette can also be used for highly specialized and for minority interest groups where open-circuit television broadcasting would be uneconomical.

If the open classroom in the informal school sometimes looks like chaos, it need not necessarily be so, provided one child or group of children is not interfering with another child or group of children. This requires sophisticated and subtle direction by the teacher. Critics feel that the open classroom will stand or fall on the basis of whether or not teachers and students have important and useful things to *do with their freedom.* If the open classroom is left to drift, then it will drift into oblivion. Videocassette technology may be used to stabilize this drift and, at times, prevent it.

The makers of hardware in the videocassette field have done little so far to assist the informalist in his educational problems. Perhaps they are afraid that, regardless of how ingenious it is, no hardware will substitute for good educational procedures. If informalists are to be successful with their procedures, it seems to us that videocassette software, like software used in more formal schooling, must pay attention to *stimulus, response* and *feedback.*

The relevant *stimulus* must be generated in terms of the student and his world. When an educational experience is inchoate, confusing, almost meaningless or unclear and distracting, the software videocassette maker may readily isolate, magnify and zoom in on an object, idea or experience that will stimulate the student. Should the stimulus be irrelevant, unarresting, dull, unimaginative or unengaging, then failure has already set in. And whether the classroom situation is informal or not will make little difference.

The videocassette maker of standardized software has a number of advantages here in the stimulus aspect of his wares. First, the television playback screen is relatively small and intimate in its communication with the viewer. The software maker, second, may take advantage of this intimate screen-scale and isolate specific ideas and experiences. The stimulus ideas and experience may be explored and repeated or developed with variations for reinforcement. The use of closeups, extreme closeups and orientation shots can reinforce learning. The still-frame picture with voice over is an added device for further stimulus enforcement. The use of color, which is at first blush merely eye-engaging, can be more than that. Color may be used to impart information in many learning situations. One need only mention art classes, botany classes and general science classes, where color is directly associated with the identification of information. Imagine in a general science class seeing on the screen a chameleon adapt itself to a variety of environmental settings as it changes its color characteristically. Here is a stimulus image so dynamic that there is little to rival it aside from the actual experience.

If the stimulus is successful, what of the *response*? What is the student supposed to have learned? Here the teacher can step in and insinuate herself into the informal situation in order to ascertain whether or not the student has indeed mastered the videocassette lesson. No formal testing is implied here—but through conversation, and cross-discussions, through application in succeeding situations of concepts taught by the cassette, the teacher can ascertain the students' apprehension, retention and learning aspects of the stimulus experience. Software might even be used to elicit student response by means of testing or doing something relevant in the application of the stimulus and then measure the degree of correctness or incorrectness of the student response via the videocassette itself.

This aspect of educational communication, of course, takes us into *feedback*. The student usually wants to know how well he did—and usually with little delay. Feedback is a guide toward further learning and the modification of learning procedures. Feedback should guide and give impact to the pacing, spacing and spreading of the teaching procedures and concepts of the stimulus and response process. Feedback may be incorporated into the pace of the videocassette itself, or it may be left to the teacher who controls the stimulus. For instance, the videocassette may communicate to the student during a geometry lesson: "If you did it correctly, your proof should look like this," and then show a closeup of the correct steps. The teacher may now stop the machine and reinforce feedback by pointing out individual errors. The student may even stop the video instrument (or hold a still frame) without the teacher in order to compare his paper with that shown on the cassette screen. The student can and should be readily able to rewind to review if feedback implies that such a review is necessary. In all stimulus-response learning situations, feedback in relevant forms, even in an informal classroom, can readily enhance the educational process. The software for this videocassette procedure must be made with care and with an eye toward this type of individualization and humanization, which, at first glance, seems to emulate the mechanization of programmed instruction but may be employed by subtle teachers and well-trained students for less rigid objectives than those usually associated with prefabricated programs.

Americans are generally impetuous. Instant reform, they tend to believe, should spell instant success. Television and radio give them instant communication. Coffee makers give them instant coffee. Automobiles and airplanes are increasing their speeds to give almost instant arrival. If instant education is expected from our schools, then we foresee inevitable disillusionment with the open classroom. Since growth, maturation and development are not instant, it follows that neither will the results of the open method of teaching be instant.

Videocassette makers for the classroom will have to experiment with many different approaches in developing the educational software required by programming and teaching. However, where the teacher in American open education is the innovator, the administrator is still, unfortunately, the buyer. The dilemma of dealing with both, who may be at odds philosophically, is the ultimate and total dilemma of the software cassette maker.

Those of us who are chosen to remind the rest of us of our madness seem to be madder then the rest. Perhaps the topsy-turvy land of Alice is our destiny, strife is our national characteristic and the innovation that is continually being born out of our failures is our only hope. Informal education and the use of the videocassette in the classroom could produce a happy marriage, but who is there who may today responsibly and certainly vouch for the normalcy of its offspring?

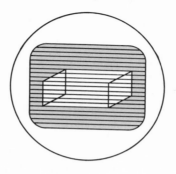

CHAPTER SIX

VIDEOCASSETTES AND THE COMPREHENSIVE HIGH SCHOOL

An adage serves to illustrate a vital point regarding the nature of the comprehensive high school: If you have a dollar and I have a dollar, and we trade, obviously nothing much is gained. Now you have a dollar, and I have a dollar, and that is that. However, if you have an idea and I have an idea, and we trade, there is necessarily much more involved. For now you have *two* ideas and I have *two* ideas. In this way, perhaps, the process of education can be served, for it seems to us that one of its essences is to quantify and then to qualify ideas, knowledge, skills and values.

Basically, the comprehensive high school is concerned with many opportunities for studying (at a relatively low level of enterprise) a great variety of subjects. According to James B. Conant, who has written widely in this field, sufficient funds are *sine qua non* for such desirable schooling. The comprehensive high school is peculiar to American education. In its curriculum, it offers to one geographical area, under one administrative roof, education to *all* the students—the academically inclined and the skills-oriented or vocationally inclined. Whereas, in other countries, curricular *selections* are made for each student at a fairly early age, in the comprehensive school the student *elects* his own curriculum after *minimal* requirements are met. This is not, then, the high school for specialists selected by authority; this is a democratic school in which all students with a heterogeneity of interests "rub shoulders" in classes in the hope, perhaps, that ideas are also traded, multiplied, quantified and qualified. Thus, the comprehensive high school attempts to provide a general education in a democratic environment, while, through its elective offerings, it provides good instruction in both the academic and vocational fields. Heterogeneity, a characteristic of the melting-pot concept of American democracy, finds its counterpart in the heterogeneity of the curriculum of the comprehensive high school. This aspect of pluralism in American democracy is reflected in the pluralism of American comprehensive high school curricula. It is both a strength and a weakness of our secondary educational world. Often, it may simply lead to quantification of superficiality instead of leading to a pursuit of quality.

In the European tradition, the selection system has often led to a nondemocratic elitism, both in schooling and in society. The American comprehensive high school basically serves a student body whose goals for education beyond the secondary level are varied.

Included in the academic curriculum of the comprehensive high school is the opportunity for two, three, or four years of study in a foreign language to achieve a modest conversational fluency in that language.

The vocational curriculum in the comprehensive high school offers opportunity for students to develop skills and attitudes that are immediately marketable upon graduation.

In such a school, there should be enough electives of a varied academic and quasi-academic nature to satisfy the career objectives of both the vocationally inclined and the academically inclined.

There exist a variety of roles for videocassette technology in the comprehensive high school. For instance, where funds for maintaining the student-teacher ratio are inadequate, a judicious use of the videocassette in a classroom situation, in a library situation, in a supervised videocassette laboratory facility, or in an independent way either at school or at home, may supersede limitations that funding imposes on the student-teacher relationship—to some degree, although it is far from a total cure for this problem. Teachers able to use with facility and with academic finesse the videocassette technology may find videocassettes the equivalent of a second teacher or teacher's aide at hand. This might well be considered a mere "second best" to the real thing for some teachers. For those pedagogically gifted with imagination and teaching skills, the videocassette might, however, prove to be *more* of a boon than a second teacher. Particularly if the software in the cassette is educationally sound and interestingly presented, then teacher supervision, lesson-plan sessions and curricular philosophy, as exemplified by a second teacher who might be balky or ineffective, evaporate as problems in the teaching situation.

With a remarkably straight face, Conant prescribes, for the ideal comprehensive high school, a regimen that allows for the teaching of calculus; that provides instruction for four years in a modern foreign language; that permits a student to study, in any one year, English, mathematics, science, a foreign language, social studies, physical education, art or music; that provides one or more advanced placement courses; and that has an average pupil load of 120 (or even

less, 100) for each teacher of English. In implementing all of
the above difficult and, to some, unrealistic suggestions,
videocassettes may be of immeasurable value. Mathematics,
calculus, language, English, social studies, art and music
should prove to be no obstacle to the videocassette producers—if they are experienced educators as well as purveyors
of enrichment. Here lies an opportunity to enhance the
educational experience of the student in a comprehensive
high school. Advanced placement courses are a "natural" for
using videocassettes, especially when coupled with the
concept of individual or independent or small-group study
for those especially gifted and qualified. Because some two
percent of the student population is what educators consider
gifted, videocassette producers may have a rich market for
their software in this type of specialized secondary education.

Currently, the political-social issue of school bussing is
tied in with the issue of equal educational opportunity for all
students. Statistics and descriptive research have revealed that
not all comprehensive high schools in the nation are equally
up to the task of providing student populations with equal
education in any conventional construction. Here lies an
opportunity for videocassettes to come to the aid of the
weaker schools, just as other specialized educational materials
have in the past. The extent and coverage of subject matter
of this software, the quality of the software content, the ease
and facility of the handling of the cassette technology to
assure wide publicity and distribution, the reasonableness of
prices (which may be kept low by wide distribution when
handled by large distributors) may help to achieve some
aspects of the type of equal educational opportunity that our
nation at large seeks to accomplish.

The authors, in preparing this chapter, have visited a

number of comprehensive high schools and have invariably found considerable discontent among the student population—and among the parents of many of the students. "My child can never get more than a few minutes' time to spend with her guidance counselor," is a typical complaint. Or: "My child is not being challenged by the pace and demands of the class. She is brighter than the rest, but the teacher spends her time with the slower students." The complaint may be vice versa: "My child is not too good in math, and she is in a section that she can't keep up with. I have to get her outside tutoring. Why can't she be changed to another section—a slower one?" These complaints are typical. Students find themselves in classes whose demands are beneath, beyond, or beside their skills, abilities, interests and goals. Slow readers, put into classes where a normal reading rate prevails, find the assignments too demanding and soon drop out physically or psychologically. Fast and gifted readers in a similar situation soon become bored with what they consider the snail's pace of learning and the minimal demands upon their abilities, and either stir up mischief or waste their time in a soporific school day.

Good counseling and the use of videocassettes may be of inestimable value in meeting these problems. Some counselors think it wise to group students into homogeneous class sections. Thus slow readers are grouped with slow readers and fast readers with fast readers. So with mathematics, science and other subjects. This is the concept of grouping the students subject by subject, according to apparent ability. Other counselors consider it more educationally sound to group brighter students, in general, with brighter students, and slower students, in general, with slower students. This is known as heterogeneous or track grouping. Educators argue that once a student is group-tracked he tends to perform in such a way as to fulfill the prophecy he thinks is implicit in his grouping. Students who are misplaced (and the numbers seem to be large, judging from our observations) find it difficult to extricate themselves from this (to them) misplacement. The results are often reflected in student and parent discontents and in poor educational results.

Counseling seems to be a crucial crossroad here. The videocassette may come to be of some assistance in either the track-grouping concept or the ability-grouping concept. If the class grouping is heterogeneous, individual student abilities may be nourished along in the same classroom by the use of cassettes tailored to the respective abilities of the students who vary for better or worse from the class norm. Where students are grouped according to ability, subject by subject, the entire class may benefit from videocassette software when exposed to a regimen meant to tax and/or improve their abilities to learn at a speed and understanding indigenous to the group.

Although the tracking system has fallen into disrepute in most educational circles, slow readers may be good in mathematics, nevertheless, and vice versa, and the videocassette may help to break the vise of this academic self-fulfilling prophecy, which has been a real and well-measured phenomenon in education (and other) experiences.

A sizeable group of students attend summer school for various reasons: to make up low grades they earned during the academic year, to take courses they could not elect during the academic year, to accelerate their educational careers, to enrich their educational experiences, to accommodate to their changed career objectives. Classes tend to be small, and studies may be individualized. Videocassettes may be one answer to both funding and teacher personnel problems in this instance.

The use of a tape facility in class which allows both the teacher and students to make their own cassettes may prove to be a stimulus to the educational process in general: As an example of what can be done with videotape, Benjamin Franklin Junior High School in Ridgewood, New Jersey, is, at this writing, making intensive use of videotaping for teaching purposes. The taping program operates under the direction of the resident audiovisual specialist. Ninth grade students, trained to operate the school's portable television cameras, video and sound tape deck and monitor, are recording more than one hundred hours of instructional programs per term. These programs, on videotape, will be played back during the school year. Projects already taped include original plays, panel discussions, gymnastic activities, mock trials in social studies classes and oral book reports in English and speech classes. Teachers throughout the school are requesting the ninth grade students to bring the television recording and playback equipment into their classrooms to record and play back the classroom activities.

Most of the teachers feel that the class will benefit from seeing their classroom efforts on the television tube. After taping, students see an immediate replay for their own analysis, evaluation and classroom discussion. According to one teacher, "The use of school-made television programs sharpens student interest and increases motivation in addition to allowing students to see themselves as others see them." Some of the teachers are using the television system to videotape their own teaching techniques by taping micro-lessons they have prepared.

Professional videocassette makers will in the future have to compete with this "homemade" cassette-making technique. Thus, the software part of the videocassette industry will find grass-roots competition a distractive fact unless quality, effectiveness and educational expertise are incorporated into the videocassette-making, as they have *not*, to date, been much in evidence in the production of most films specifically made for the educational market.

As noted above, the comprehensive high school is peculiarly an American phenomenon springing directly from American idealism concerning a broad base of educational opportunities for all youngsters, regardless of their particular talents. Unlike various European secondary educational systems which are, one way or another, selective and specialized, with a fixed curriculum, the American system is elective and offers a variety of courses for a variety of youth. The comprehensive high school attempts to serve differing interests, desires and goals. It services those who wish to go directly from high school into a job; and it also services those who intend to continue an academic course in college and perhaps in graduate school.

It has been—and will continue to be—criticized by many at home and abroad for attempting to do too much, often shoddily, while it might serve our nation better if it were less comprehensive and set itself to teaching well fewer subjects. In many ways, the criticism is gratuitous, as long as we conceive of secondary education as being at the same time a vocational, cultural and college preparatory institution. It is a condition, far from a perfect one, of American idealism and our notions of freedom of opportunity for the young.

Its critics—whose nostalgia and sentiment may be admired and even sympathized with—are dodging the real social issues comprehensive schools attack by hiding behind semantic clouds of "high standards" and "basic education" that are realistically irrelevant to the present and future needs of most American children. Special aspirations and special talents may be met in special schools, public and/or private, and the progress of such schools should be encouraged. But they are quite beside the *point* of the comprehensive high school and *its* peculiar problems.

Because the range and variety of course offerings is a characteristic of the comprehensive high school (with the freedom to elect course offerings within the academic or vocational areas) and because the opportunities exist for individual advanced study both for gifted and non-gifted students, videocassette software can and should play an important role in the educational curricula of comprehensive high schools. Diversified course offerings may be unusually enriched by a good resource library of readily accessible videocassettes and simple, easy-to-handle playback technology.

The videocassette soft- and hardware enthusiasts will soon be attempting to introduce this new technology to the public by way of the avenues of business, government and education. If the cassette industry begins to acquire the characteristics of professional equipment wherein it is precise, dependable and flexible enough to adapt to variant situations, then public interest in cassette technology will begin to awaken on a national level. The ability of professional software experts to produce individualized learning-video-cassette experiences to which students will respond favorably will be influenced to a large degree by the control the teacher and/or student will be able to maintain over the medium, a control, or lack of it, that explains much both about the successes and failure of technology in American education. Hence, the need for simplified operation of origination and playback technology in the videocassette field as well as continual sensitivity to the different needs of different teachers in different types of schools. In addition to simplification and standardization of operation, the interchanging of videocassettes among classrooms, schools and school systems seems to us to be a prerequisite to the catalyzing of the entire industry into ready acceptance by the educational world. Other characteristics that will enhance the use of videocassettes in the comprehensive high schools center upon the flexibility of the device, that should include: still frame, slow motion and reasonably good electronic editing; print-out of sequences on stills from the video-cassettes (resembling Xerography) for deeper study; easy and cheap duplication methodology for widest use of cassettes; the ability to create special effects such as split frames and overlays; random access devices; reasonably priced high speed duplication technology; low costs for home-brewed origination of videocassettes; and uncomplicated maintenance both for black and white and for color cassettes in origination and playback equipment.

Resistance to change and innovation forever face a society whose institutions "work." Let us set up a hypothetical equation here which we caution the reader not to take without challenge: in most cases, the degree of radicalness in the innovative change will be directly proportionate to the degree of resistive tenacity with which the innovation is by-and-large met. Videocassette technology is an innovative change. It will be challenged by the educational filmmakers, by the textbook world, and by film-slide and blackboard and chalk and pencil and paper notebook manufacturers, among others. Teachers themselves, who forever fear obsolescence on the horizon, will certainly resist the innovation. Yet, to our way of seeing videocassette technology, it is neither revolutionary nor is it innovative enough to change fundamentally or drastically American education. Nor will any competent teacher's job be threatened by it.

Videocassette technology is no panacea for the profound and numerous problems of education. It is simply an added device (or encumbrance, whichever way you choose at the moment to look at it) that may make education richer, or poorer, depending upon how it is used, when and where. Oversell of innovation in education is not the fundamental problem we have with the videocassette, the main reason, we believe, for the general failure of Instructional TV. The problem is to ascertain the potential of the videocassette and to see to it that it does not simply become just one more piece of elaborate wreckage on the historical path of educational evolutionary technology and methodology.

The comprehensive high school is fertile soil for the software videocassette makers. One cassette used successfully will almost inevitably induce the utilization of a second; and a second cassette the using of a third, and so on. It adds up to the fact that if you have a dollar and I have a dollar, and we trade, little is gained. We each have a dollar. However, if you have a cassette and I have a cassette, and we trade, now you have two complexes of ideas, and I have two complexes of ideas, and our appetites are hopefully whetted for more and more and more, if the ideas are quantified and qualified with imagination, excitement, authority and educational expertise. Opportunity is knocking.

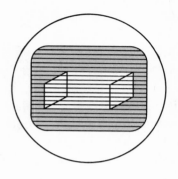

CHAPTER SEVEN

OPEN ENROLLMENT AND THE "NEW COLLEGE"

Since the crack of the egg and the emergence of what is known today as "Audiovisual Education" from the era of lantern slides and Keystone silent films, up to the present moment of Rand-type strategists kneading brows and welding space technology into instructional systems by means of "think-tank" gobbledygook, two major sins have consistently run through the particular cultural and educational curiosity called today "Educational Technology."

One is a conservative sin; the other, one of excess.

On the conservative side, the neglect of potential savings of time and talent by means of technical "know-how," and, in certain instances, the genuine improvement of much teaching and learning by the same technology need not be extenuated for the readers of this volume. The culprit here is that academic elf (born of the necessity for proper custodians for school technology and an over-supply of physical and vocational education teachers) who was (and still often is) known in many schools as the resident "AV creep."

Not quite able to fix a broken projector, tape recorder

or TV set, this "specialist" is forever on the prowl in the halls of our schools and colleges. Thoroughly sold on some absurd mystique, lately—and inarticulately—the one espoused by Dr. McLuhan and his gulls, he tries to find gaps in conventional instructional procedures into which to cram films, records, projectuals and other frequently irrelevant goodies, much to the distaste, usually, of those teachers whose business is teaching and of those students who may want to learn enough to pass their exams. For all the fancy and high-priced texts that are sold on this arcane art, the "creep" remains a comparatively silent, and somewhat unwelcome, outsider in most of our schools and universities, tolerated but rarely cherished—if he is lucky.

The sin of excess has taken the form of a glut of well-meant promises—promises that for the past generation have emerged from the mouths of educators involved in communications technology, *not one of which* has been fulfilled in fact, in the most liberal construction imaginable—with the possible exception of teaching foreign pronunciation by means of recordings, in instances where live language instructors were not competent to pronounce correctly the tongue they were teaching. (At present, if you want to learn a foreign language—and you can afford it—you do not fool with tapes or records if you are smart, nor do you study the subject in school. You trot off to Berlitz or a similar academy and get yourself a living teacher who gives you a "crash course" in the language eight hours a day, six days a week. In a dozen days, you will be speaking and comprehending a serviceable but primitive Arabic or Chinese like a native, if you pay attention.)

And *what* promises! Education by television; Visual Literacy; history relived in the classroom; *new* reading techniques—and *remedial* reading techniques for those who had been exposed to the *new* reading techniques; "Talking Typewriters" creating child prodigies; literature and English taught by film, revolution in skill building, attitude formation, discipline problems, use of teaching talent, etc., etc., etc.! Oversell, overkill or sabotage—put the blame where you will—audiovisual education has made enormous promises to our schools and educators for the past generation, and it is still making them. But if all the educational technology in the nation were proscribed by law tomorrow, most students and teachers in most of our schools would hardly notice the difference. In fact, many administrators and education board members might hail such a move as a brave and ingenious "innovation" in schooling! Nor would they be entirely wrong.

One wonders why.

In sober reappraisal, and despite their occasional childishness, the "AV creeps" *did* have something to offer their fellow teachers, and sometimes it was effective educationally—but all too infrequently. At least half of the technological innovations that were supposed to revolutionize schooling *did* offer mild potentials at least to improve it. What went wrong? And why?

This is not the place to chart or reconsider this history. Others have already done it, bravely attempting to pump into their narratives a little nitrous oxide for what is essentially a sad story.

The establishment in education (meaning those teachers and administrators on the firing line) simply saw no need for methodological alternatives to what they were doing, according to their criteria, quite well in their classrooms. And they did not wish to place in jeopardy their roles as teachers and administrators by turning over to some novel form of instrumentation a function they presently performed. Not all the cozy, intimate counsel at faculty meetings, not all the propaganda ignited in schools of education, not all the influence of professional organizations or bribes by private entrepreneurs could move them much. Nor will it tomorrow. In this respect, teachers and administrators are like tailors, bartenders, airline stewardesses, concert pianists, night-club entertainers and croupiers. While all of them *may be* somehow replaced by instruments of technology, none of them *will be*—in any degree—until they *have to be.* Then they will retreat or vanish *only* at the behest of dire necessity.

Today a new necessity, however, confronts American education, most particularly higher education. While every effort will be made to meet it *without* the use of technology, and in conventional ways, the job is simply too staggering and too immense to yield to conventional solutions in practice. At this point, the "AV creep" and "educational technologist" will suddenly discover that he is an extremely important person. If he is then incapable of rising to the challenge in front of him—and he may well be—he will be dismissed out of hand, and the specific conditions that opened his new opportunity will be transposed from the "necessity" column of educational priorities to the "unnecessary" one, and peace will be restored, but at quite a price.

Specifically, the pressure is that of open enrollment to our colleges and the proliferation of one- and two-year junior and community colleges that are placing—and will continue to place—ever-increasing stresses upon the entire educational community in our country.

The causes of the pressures are obvious and simple: higher education, or at least the introductory aspects of it, is no longer an educational "frill" for an elite or for selective beneficiaries of our culture. It is rapidly, for better or worse, taking the place of what a high-school diploma stood for a quarter of a century ago. Within the authors' lifetime, they have seen higher education (or education beyond the senior year of high school) metamorphosed from a *privilege* (albeit frequently an unfairly distributed one) granted to a tiny fraction of the populace to a *right* exercised by what is fast becoming a majority of it.

To accommodate this stress, of course, higher education, as Jencks and Riesman have shown in *The Academic Revolution,* and the very nature of the concept of schooling beyond secondary school had also to change (and is, at this moment, changing) in the process. We are not concerned here with the exact nature of the change or its social ramifications, matters treated by others beyond our competences. Suffice it to say that an old vision of liberal higher education—sweet as it was—as articulated by men like Clark Kerr, Harold Taylor and A.N. Whitehead is moribund, if not dead, a necessary sacrificial step taken in order to achieve, we hope, the civilization and acculturation of new masses of students continuing beyond high school. This is not to say that the kind of education these scholars bespoke is now but a memory; it fortunately remains with us, and will probably remain into the future—but it is no longer either an inevitable or a desirable set of objectives for a large proportion of our young people in institutions of higher education who have good and highly practical reasons for moving into our colleges and sub-colleges. What *has* changed is not the adequacy of this vision *for a minority of college students,* but the social setting and pragmatic pressures *being placed at this moment* upon our universities and colleges to abandon this ideal for the majority of their student population.

Granting this new constituency, its *new* needs are: a modest introduction into the liberal arts, development of skill in English, a wide-ranging and necessary purview of the social and behavioral sciences, as well as some perfunctory exploration in the fine arts, differentially offered according to their individual aspirations. *Second in importance* is the mastery of some sort of technological skill (repairing television sets, hotel management, medical and dental assistance and so forth). This new constituency is neither interested in nor competent to face our new colleges (or old ones with doors wide open), if these institutions merely replicate those old colleges that preceded them by enlarging their scope and lowering their standards. What they require is an entirely *new* sort of college. And herein lies both a problem and a challenge.

What sort of college is a new college? And, if its essential quality is changed to meet new and hitherto unconsidered needs of new types of students, is it still a college? The latter question is a semantic trap and a nice subject for arguments between weepers with large towels. Moans and groans at the prospect and necessity of open-admissions college enrollments are totally nonproductive. Society has simply changed and moved faster than the keepers of the higher academic flame. Open enrollment—and everything it stands for—is rapidly, on a nationwide basis, becoming ancient history. The future, however, still contains the answer to the question of what will become of it.

The first concern above is a sensible one, and here the educational technologist *does not yet* have meaningful or proper answers. But he may point the *way* to some possible answers; and, in so doing, produce genuine justification for his existence for the first time in the history of American education, so many, many years after he first brought his magic lantern projector into the schoolhouse.

First, let us consider what the new college (or new parts of old colleges) *will not* and *cannot* be and *cannot* do. It

cannot offer enormous undergraduate lecture courses of a
survey nature in the arts and sciences, assuming even that
students are sufficiently motivated to suffer antique professors reading to them their time-worn lecture notes, without
falling asleep, deserting the lecture hall, rioting out of sheer
boredom or complaining and protesting loudly that they are
victims of a grand deception. Neither may proliferated
sections of small groups (Section A, Section B, Section C,
remember?) join eager, bright-eyed graduate students in
emulating Socrates, chewing in informal class encounters a
senior professor's or textbook's copious wisdom concerning
Western Civilization, Introductory Sociology or *The Literature of the West.* Graduate students are rarely much good at
this sort of teaching, because it takes enormous skill, and it is
doubtful that even our largest universities are able to produce
enough of them even marginally competent to handle the
multiple seminars that swollen enrollments are producing.

Second, what is the alternative? The new college has to
be, in one respect or another, an efficient instrument to
process masses of students in certain basic studies at a level of
effectiveness somewhat below our former aspirations for
university scholarship. Does this mean that it is destined to
become a "factory" (not a new charge for many large
old-style universities), or that its euphemistic "high standards" must be compromised? Of course, this is precisely what
it means! But, taken alone, neither eventuality implies that
the institution involved or higher education in general will be
hurled along the road to doom or extinction. If these courses
of study are offered, described and given exactly as, and for,
what they are—understood not to duplicate in content or
style older, similar courses, but instead designed to meet the
specific and honest needs of a new constituency—neither the
university institution nor the old ideals of higher education

need suffer, be diminished or be trivialized. And, while it may send shivers down the spines of their collective alumni as they gasp in the tap rooms of their respective University Clubs, this truism applies equally as directly to Yale, Harvard, Dartmouth and Princeton as to the Universities of Nevada, Nebraska, Alaska or Hawaii, and other more or less proletarian schools like City College of New York as well as large, eccentric private universities supposedly operating in the public interest.

The way that the educational technologist or "AV creep" may gently lead his professional colleagues into this alternative and out of the nettles and barbs it contains is most definitely *not* the way he has been traditionally traveling to date. That is, he will not help to solve their problems by doing what he has been attempting to do for many years: either "enriching" present instruction with various sound and picture gadgets he incorrectly calls "media," or simply recording on film or TV tape present instruction as it is currently offered, stimulating it a bit with electronic razzle-dazzle, or trotting out a new vocabulary of pseudo-technical terms like "input," "output," "entropy" and "information"—silly words, all drawn from (and misused in) the rich and fanciful grunt-language of systems engineering.

No, indeed. The approach which he has the opportunity to introduce into our colleges—if he is competent to embark upon so daring a journey—must begin where *all* fundamental revision of education must begin, and which almost all current efforts at school reform overlook, and therefore fail. The first task centers not upon methods of teaching or modifications of old patterns of presenting to students what was formerly considered basic college education, but upon *content*. Until the question is clearly answered concerning exactly what open enrollment *is supposed to accomplish in the matter of course content during the first two years of college*—when it will presumably terminate schooling for some and send others on to advanced work—all other solutions to the problems created by our new colleges are irrelevant and wastes of time and energy. Education may as well be picking flowers or playing chess if we have not decided precisely what it is we want this new breed of student to be taught. Note that we are not referring here to *objectives* or what students will *learn*, but what is actually *taught*!

What is this *content* to contain, begging all essentially divisive questions concerning how its ends are achieved? In the absence of any generally accepted clear answers, let us offer these specific suggestions, severing them, for the moment, from the supposed stated aims, goals and objectives of education that our present colleges are supposed to be reaching, and whatever it is that colleges are presently doing, or whatever it is that professors *think* they are doing right now.

Briefly, the two years should contain, aside from whatever technical or professional content is demanded from them:

1) Mature study of the use of the English language, in contemporary contexts preferably, as manifest in fiction, drama, poetry and expository essays. This content and curriculum should be both analytical and creative in nature, with one end in view: to provide for normal students adult skills in reading profitably and writing clearly. Speech and hortatory expressiveness are secondary issues here. *Too much attention,* it seems to the authors, is these days given to verbal encounters and rhetoric both inside and out of school.

2) The study of recent history as it bears upon the

American experience today, with a heavy concentration upon foreign policy, the role of technology in society, recent experiences of *all* minority groups in America and elsewhere, the nature and development of mass culture, as well as basic facts concerning the political structures of the major modern States, should also be required.

3) Recent developments in the behavioral and social sciences, particularly the former (as an antidote to the faddism in which they are enveloped in the popular mind), should also be covered. Here, contemporary problems of drug addiction, alcoholism, mass apathy, mental illness and other indices of modern anomie, as they apply to life, must be ruthlessly examined, along with their handmaiden, popular culture as spread by newspapers, films, radio and television.

4) Natural science, centering mostly upon an intensive inquiry into the contemporary by-products of technology that only scientific inquiry and solutions will ameliorate— problems like ecology, pollution, depletion of natural re- sources, overpopulation, etc.—must also be treated objective- ly. The main aim of this specific inquiry is to understand both the *nature* and *limits* of science, its role in modern life and how, where and why it cleaves from technology.

These four areas ("core studies" or "basic inquiries") should, at least, be required of *all* students entering into two-year programs, not, however, as discrete "courses" in the usual manner of contemporary higher education. If they are reduced [sic] to this level of discourse, we may as well forget them and return to English I, Social Science II and the other dreary nonsense that presently fills most college bulletins.

Nor should these areas be systematized and programmed into neat packages that assume that all students—even masses of them—have the same interests, needs or abilities. Grades for these studies are also irrelevant. If they are needed for future purposes in further schooling, by all means grades should be given to those students who want them. If they are not needed, however, they should be ruthlessly eliminated and certificates or records of accomplishment or non-accomplishment (call them "P" and "F" or "X" and "Y," if you wish) should constitute *the total pay-off for the student*, aside from what he has learned.

Now, how is this end to be accomplished? While much of the technology involved is still in inchoate form, the following suggestions may be adapted to many courses of study in many ways. The *division of enterprise* that they bespeak is, however, the *only* critical aspect to their accomplishment in meeting the needs of the new university.

1) *All* exposition of subject matter material should be utilized by and under the control of the student himself. Periodic examinations of an objective nature will indicate both to him and his instructors what he has been up to. The spine of instruction should be relegated to videocassettes that are issued to students, and which may be viewed, reviewed and studied at the student's leisure, either in mass viewing centers consisting of multiple, soundproofed, comfortable viewing carrels (similar to today's language laboratories) or, preferably (and if the technology is available) in students' dormitories or their own homes. Where visual materials are not necessary, audiocassettes will suffice. The operational word here is "spine," and it is meant to substitute in large part for what we consider today in university education "classroom instruction" or "lectures," the hub upon which most college courses still turn. The *exact* nature of this software unfortunately cannot be determined at this time. It will depend, naturally, upon the course of study, the institution using it, the students involved and the pool of instructional ability available to the college at any time. It

will obviously constitute a mix of prefabricated software on one hand ("educational media," if you like the term) and specialized, home-grown instruction designed both to meet the individual requirements of those students who use it and to emphasize immediate and contemporaneous references of the subject at hand, no matter what it is. Its preparation will probably be relegated to a University Cassette Production Center that will produce, modify and edit these video-cassettes in close cooperation with the academic divisions or departments responsible for both their learning strategy and content. Ultimate responsibility for them—and decisions concerning when and how to discard and/or change them—*must ultimately rest in academic hands, not* at the convenience, whim, or judgments of educational specialists or garden-variety college administrators.

2) Expository materials should *all* be custom-made to fit the needs of the particular students following *one* particular educational path in *one* particular institution at *one* particular time. In other words, all recorded material should be created, edited or organized *locally* by each college itself—*and completely erased and updated each semester,* in the spirit of the BBC's practical twenty-year experience with in-school broadcasting in Britain. Non-locally originated segments of newsreels, speeches, lectures, films and TV shows may, of course, be integrated *ad lib* into these videocassettes. But, under no circumstances should they merely constitute miniature duplications of today's so called "university film libraries" (most of the stock of which is invariably and hopelessly out of date). Unlike the British, American educational technologists (particularly TV and filmmakers) have been willing to rest content with "solutions" to academic problems, rather than regarding *any* tape, film, or educational instrument as but a *step* towards instructional

perfection that can and will never be reached and *must* always—with the passage of time—be open to both continual upgrading and improvement. Any college videocassette technology that operates on the assumption—as the educational film industry does today—that a specific film or piece of software is ever finally "finished" (or that it is entirely satisfactory for educational purposes on any but the crudest skill-teaching level) will defeat both the spirit and nature of what the new college—as the Open University in Britain and the BBC's in-school broadcasts by radio and TV have now demonstrated beyond a doubt—should strive to be. In some ways, the challenge to meet this particular *requirement* of videocassette technology on the college level may prove to be *the single most difficult one* that both subject matter specialists *and* educational technologists may have to stand up to in the years to come. But face it, they will. And it will remain critical to the successes or failures of their efforts.

3) *No* conventional textbooks of any sort should be utilized in the program. (They mold the student to their, almost invariably, obsolete and peculiar conventions, rather than permit the student options of choice, for better and worse, in following his own curiosity and talent.) Cheap, paperback non-texts may satisfy some former textbook functions, particularly in the English language "content program" (for lack of a better word). But even *they* should run second in utility to Xeroxed, written and graphic materials (and, of course, multiple videocassettes) specifically designed to lead the student through the content of each one of the tracks at his own pace and in his own way.

4) Classroom seminars may be employed in handling, explaining and discussing the expository materials in the videocassettes (as well as trouble-shooting them for defects to be changed or eliminated) and assigning student projects

and individual research work. But such group meetings are dangerous. A two-hour "encounter-like" seminar is invariably less effective and meaningful educationally than a ten-minute interview with a skilled instructor—for the student, not the instructor, although it may be less therapeutic for both. If instructors (or *intelligent* graduate students) are in short supply, a scheme might be devised whereby students instruct and guide *each other* through well-defined projects and assignments, perhaps charging a second-year student with assisting a freshman in his studies, or—why not?—vice versa. Students on the same level may, also profitably, guide and direct one another's efforts as well as view and discuss videocassettes together. If teams of brighter students are desirable to match-up, a computer may locate and pair compatible pupils. If incompatibilities are desired (a more fruitful notion, we suggest), the same computer can search them out also.

5) Students who do not exhibit the *desire* to learn and direct their own inquiries in a reasonable and honest manner and take advantage of the educational "spine" offered by their videocassettes should be ruthlessly weeded out of the "new college" and sent either to work or to a trade school—as dramatically and openly as possible. Perhaps it is wise to allow committees of open-enrollment students to make these somewhat sensitive decisions themselves, rather than trusting to the wisdom of teachers and administrators, whose predictive capacities often prove faulty. The main factors in this matter should be *motivation* and *accomplishment*, in about a fifty-fifty mix. Conventional academic standards of accomplishment simply will not apply to the essential goals of this type of program, or to the means employed to achieve its ends.

The suggestions above are merely offered as crude

methodological guidelines, but they are critical, we think, to the major problem that the "new college" will have to face: preventing it from falling back into the tried and tired matrix of conventional early undergraduate schooling as we have come to know it and in the face of the opportunities offered by today's videocassette technology.

The "revolutionary" scheme outlined above is, all in all, at heart extremely *reactionary,* as the sophisticated reader has already probably observed. In the context of *today's* problems and today's technologies of education (mainly videocassettes and Xerography), it is a close replication of what university education once accomplished in Europe, England and the United States during most of the past century. Itinerant scholars, resident professors and various hangers-on created a "university community" where one was free to follow his natural curiosities and meet his own peculiar educational needs by means of contact both with his peers (as ignorant and confused, frequently, as they were) and various scholars who had mastered the disciplines they assayed—as well as having access to a good number of manuscript libraries and other modern (to them) "media." The term "academic freedom," in fact, was derived from this context and type of education—not the freedom of an *instructor* to say what he pleased (a freedom *no* teacher anywhere has ever had, or has today), but the freedom of the *student* to search as widely and as deeply as his disposition and skill permitted into the various disciplines available for his scrutiny. And he was given as well the precious and inevitable freedom to fail as miserably as he wished, if he lacked motivation, brains or sticking power, without undue disgrace or social opprobrium.

Such complete freedom is, of course, not a realistic paradigm for the college education of the masses of poorly and semi-educated youngsters who are flowing into our open enrollment institutions today. They have not been prepared for it; nor are the times and circumstances right for it. But the spirit, if not the letter, of a former age when education was a privilege and a prize may yet return to our colleges—thanks to modern technology and the awesome prospect of open enrollment in college for all who want it, rather than those who can afford it, or have been deemed, by arbitrary and often faulty criteria, fit for it. We may yet, therefore, achieve in the United States a new and worthy construction of the ill-used term "academic freedom" by virtue, largely, of the new technology of videocassettes.

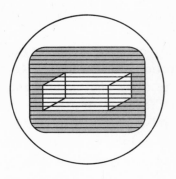

CHAPTER EIGHT

VIDEOCASSETTES AND ADULT EDUCATION

America leads the world in Adult Education.

For the uninitiated in the oddities of schooling, this is *not* a phrase that is likely to make professors of Adult Education happy. But the facts of the matter are beyond dispute. Almost any issue of any popular magazine or Sunday Supplement will provide advertisements for a dazzling display of self-improvement *courses*—ranging all the way from art appreciation to improved sex techniques—available (for cash) from correspondence schools, or lessons on phonograph records and tape or various types of apparently ingeniously programmed instruction. All of this uplift is invariably surrounded by copy-writers' purple prose explaining how this or that technique will teach adults, in their full senses we assume, to beat the odds on Wall Street, to play the piano without even trying or to develop a vocabulary to rival that of Spiro Agnew.

And then there are *the books.* Talk to any man or woman in the mass-market book business and he will tell you that almost any volume, the title of which begins with "How

To," is a potential best-seller and gold mine. Such works are, in fact, known in the trade as "How-Tos," and certain professional scribes write nothing but such works, even and especially on subjects they know little about—at least when they start writing. Presumably, they are "How To" experts, and the particular art, skill or technique to which they address themselves is more or less irrelevant to their expository skills. (A former female colleague of both present writers wrote an endless number of "How To" sex books and cook books. Her advanced years precluded much recent—we assume—experience with the former; and, to the best of our knowledge, she usually ate in restaurants.)

The market for "How Tos" is not just enormous, it is literally *fantastic,* involving book clubs and mail-order schemes. And "How To" books cover the entire range of human possibilities: how to practice witchcraft; how to raise mushrooms in your cellar; how to cure your own hay fever; how to turn garbage into lighting fixtures; how to *lose* money on investments (yes!); how to get rid of your spouse; and other topics that literally stagger one's capacity for underestimating the gullibility of the reading (or book-buying) public.

Then, there is the matter of *classes.* Accurate estimates of the percentage of our adult population who trot off, at least one day or night a week, to classes in something are hard to come by, but nobody who has studied the matter would be surprised by an estimate as large as twenty-five percent. Classes are provided for cultural uplift ("great" books, "great" speeches, "great" painting and/or "great" everything), skill development (often titled *Write That Novel, Paint Your Own House* or some such promising rubric), or for a mixture of curiosity and the desire for self-improvement (psychology courses are probably the current favorites in this mode) as well as other courses, difficult to qualify: painting for the non-artist, marionette workshops, writers' seminars for illiterates and encounter groups which offer merely to expand one's consciousness. Also notable are problem-oriented courses that settle in detail—and frequently *ad nauseam*—on whatever specific social evils are in cultural vogue at the time. At the present moment, courses in drug addiction and ecology are sure winners. But styles change fast in social problems.

Why do people take these courses? There is no sense in circumlocuting or pussyfooting. About half are professional, chronic students or teachers collecting Brownie Points that will either move them up the ladder towards a degree or give them inaptly named "inservice" credits towards promotions or pay raises. The other half are just bored adults, turned off by movies made for kids, sick of television, who want to get away from hearth, home and family for a few hours and to make social contacts, difficult to come by if you are advanced in years and do not like nursing drinks in cocktail lounges and roadhouses.

Taken together, the total number of adults occupied in one way or another in this broader *apercu* of Adult Education must therefore be formidable. Half of our population would not be an unreasonable conservative estimate to some.

When one encounters experts and professionals in Adult Education, however, one also encounters an almost inevitable malaise and many discontents—dispositions, stated or implied, that Adult Education as a national institution is not all it should be. Quite clearly, the problem of these experts cannot be quantitative. Adult Education is one of the largest (and possibly most prosperous) *businesses* in the nation, if one looks at it entirely through quantitative blinders and concentrates on sheer volume and activity. What, then, is the problem, and why do Adult Education authorities fill learned journals with articles that drip unspoken assumptions that schooling given to grownups is a challenge to be met, rather than a promise that has been fulfilled?

The answer, of course, is (as it should be) qualitative. What irks the professionals is neither our adult population's apparent thirst for self-improvement, nor their avidity for quenching that thirst, but the nature, first, of what they regard as education, and, second, the quality of what is offered to them. In these discontents they are dead right. And, if they are not discontented, they ought to be.

Certain facts of the matter loom large, and they are antecedent to any projection of the role that videocassettes may—and hopefully will—play in remedying these realistic discomforts.

Fact number one is that, in our affluent, free-enterprise system, Adult Education of certain kinds may be extremely profitable for clever businessmen who know something about mass marketing and possess sufficient nerve to back up their convictions with mass advertising. The book publishers involved are sharp specialists, and their genius lies less in advertising their wares (their market will often seek them out) than in properly distributing them.

Most correspondence schools are quasi-con-games, and so are printed programmed lessons, tapes and records that require both slick and specialized advertising on exactly the *right* outlets (*certain* magazines, *certain* radio or television programs, *certain* well-honed and selected mailing lists, etc.) as well as facilities for mass distribution, usually provided (with taxpayers' subsidies) by the Post Office.

Privately operated schools for adults—sometimes associated with more-or-less legitimate private colleges, schools and universities—may also be extremely profitable enterprises.

The father of one of America's most distinguished educational historians made his million during the depression running a chain of second-story music "schools," offering "lessons" for twenty-five cents apiece—along with use of an instrument. A rinky-dink technological institute (which defined "technology" as anything that more than six people would take a course in) started less than a generation ago in an urban slum loft. Today it boasts a grandiose campus in a fashionable suburb.

The secret of these successes is quite simple: fast turnover of students, low overhead and coolie wages for teachers, particularly foreign nationals who teach language courses (almost entirely in their own language and hence "audio-linguistically") because they cannot speak English and are grateful to work even for pennies. Out-of-work office managers and secretaries are available almost as freely—and cheaply—to teach "secretarial skills" and alphabetic stenography. Former airline hostesses and models abound in most cities and suburbs to teach almost anything—including the art of travel and vacationing. And genuine *teachers* (whose recent salary schedules have moved many from the one-time near-necessity of moonlighting in the world of Adult Education) are frequently willing to take on a few adult classes for a modest stipend, particularly if they play the ponies or fool with stocks and bonds. The underbelly of this world, in short, is far from savory, but it *is* legal, and, for those who collect the profits, highly lucrative.

Fact number two is that the aspirations of many adults—and here we are speaking both generally and broadly—are not very exacting or specific. Few of them are ready to bring any but modest labors to their pursuits of uplift. To get them actually to *read* the books in a Great Books course is difficult; they would rather discuss, criticize or listen to a teacher talk *about* them. To induce adults involved in a creative writing course actually to *write* anything longer than a paragraph is frequently something of a chore, to say nothing of trying to get them to *rewrite* a former effort. Nor do such students, in fact (and in their defense), actually know enough about any discipline to realize when and how completely a glib but shallow teacher may bamboozle them. Thus, rehashed book reviews pass for literary criticism; paperback popularizations of Freud pose as child and adolescent psychology; bits and jots of wisdom culled from think-pieces in *Life* and the *Reader's Digest* are palmed off as philosophy; and so forth—and nobody is any, practically speaking, apparently the worse for it. An incompetent, shallow teacher has turned a dollar, and his or her students subsequently glow with illusory enlightenment.

What much (or most) Adult Education boils down to might, therefore, be called "meta-education": in fact, the teaching and learning of the terms of discourse and surface concerns of a subject, but rarely an investigation of the subject itself. Present programming on public television (another ubiquitous form of all-pervasive adult hankering after trappings rather than substance) is unfortunately replete with such superficiality, meta-teaching and meta-learning, more clearly and less hypocritically offered than by mail or in school because of the strictures of telecasting's time and circumstances. One may, for instance, after exposure to a few telecourses on the American transcendental poets, talk learnedly (and quickly) about Longfellow, Thoreau, Emerson *et al.*—without having read a word of their works. A panel discussion on the issue of press freedom regarding the relatively recent "Pentagon Papers" provides ammunition for an individual to discourse with apparent intelligence about "freedom of speech," armed merely with the foggiest notion of its role in Constitutional and/or juridical history, either in our country or anywhere else.

In effect, Adult Education (and both commerical and noncommercial educational broadcasters have been culprits here) has accordingly enfranchised a great portion of our (mostly) middle class citizenry—whose motives, incidentally, are entirely benign—into extraordinarily eloquent meta-experts: that is, experts on being expert about almost anything; anything, that is, that has been portentously and superficially treated by the mass Adult Education machine. Aside from the potential threat that this sort of chicanery holds out for democracy by undermining what is left of our Jeffersonian idealism concerning an "enlightened electorate," it is also a real and insidious form of cruelty, because a moment of truth regarding one's ignorance of what one *thought* one knew is inevitable if the game continues long enough. In fact, Adult Education, so practiced, reverses the possibility of any single individual's attempt to grasp a vision of the ideal state of wisdom for which Socrates searched: the sweet knowledge that one indeed does not *know* anything very clearly or well, and is therefore wise both to recognize and accept his limitations, first, and to attempt, second, to suffer the pain of destroying his own euphoria by actually learning something.

The great canard, therefore, of Adult Education, pervading almost every nook and cranny of it, is the many-faceted illusion that "learning is fun," or, if not "fun" in a childish sense, at least fashionable, smart, chic and defensible for its own sake. And, if not learning itself, then the *illusion* of being learned—of having mastered the *right* vocabulary to talk the patois of sociology, for instance; to drop the names of the *right* scholars and to imply that one has read the *right* books and mastered the *right* issues to discuss intelligently (and here the word is used so broadly as to cover merely "intelligibility") a significant issue in an academic, or quasi-academic, field.

In his famous essay on the subject in *Teacher in America*, Jacques Barzun has discussed this cultural phenomenon at length, considering both the causes and effects of "popular teaching" in their many and horrible dimensions with a detachment and *savior-faire* that the present writers envy. What Barzun wrote years ago is all the more relevant today, first, because of the present ubiquity of serious or "educational" television (excluding that portion of it directed at school classrooms) and second, because of the *potential* market for videocassettes, which *portend a new, lucrative and enormous public for exactly the kind of Adult Education that has been such a qualitative disaster during the past generation.*

One does not need to be a Jules Verne to grasp the possibilities held out by the latter. The very nonsense that public relations flacks for educational software presently employ to peddle their merchandise indicates clearly what is just around the corner—unless stopped by miracle or muscle. Extensive distribution and/or duplication outlets for videocassettes (either utilizing erasable tape or cheap plastic or film) will, indeed, bring to the adult consumer—in his own home at his convenience—the much touted "great heritage of the past," "the knowledge and wisdom of the present" and every wacky prognostication for the future that our so-called great minds are able to conceive, in full color, one supposes, and not too expensively. In fact, anything and everything that has ever been filmed, recorded or placed on videotape may fall easily within the reach of anybody who wants it, conveniently and at a reasonable price. If enough people grab at these materials, also, the price will be very *low* and the profits unbelievable.

In corporation suites and advertising agencies, this eventuality is a most cheerful prospect. In fact, it is joyous to anyone who regards the adult public as a "market" and is fundamentally concerned with separating people from their money. From the educator's viewpoint—particularly the Adult Educator's—it is, conservatively speaking, the portent of a mixed blessing at best, and doom at worst. He knows, for instance, that the "wisdom of the ages" has been available in cross-indexed collections of books, sold as packages, for decades, and that hundreds of thousands of such repositories have been sold by seductive advertising to gullible consumers, but with little tangible result despite their circulation. He knows, also, that the mere ownership of a superb encyclopedia is more a matter of status-building than scholarship for ninety-nine out of one hundred people who fall for the ego-expanding traps of eager, well-trained encyclopedia salesmen. In truth, the very glut of information these packages of collective wisdom contain is the major factor that *prevents* them from ever making much of an impression upon the people who own them and take such pleasure in the impressive display of their bindings in their bookcases.

Videocassette technology has the power to compound this phenomenon to absurdity and beyond. Without a doubt, the adult home market for educational videotapes will be potentially enormous, *if* that market can be identified, solicited properly and organized into an entity whereby software may be distributed to it as rapidly as it can be gobbled up. The quantitative growth—and success, from the corporation suite viewpoint—of Adult Education in the West and a new apotheosis of it is therefore almost assured by the development of videocassette technology. Adult Education, in the broadest construction of the term, is likely to advance from the highly lucrative business it is today into a *fantastically* lucrative one tomorrow. With videocassettes easily and cheaply available by mail, suitable for adult interests in "uplift" (the only term that will describe the aim of the development), at computerized "dubbing stations" or by carrier cable, it is probable that, in a decade or two, one-half to two-thirds of our adult population will be in some manner engaged physically in Adult Educational activities— some still in school, some still taking correspondence courses, but the lion's share of them glowing with enrichment in their own homes in front of video tubes (or screens) fed by cassettes of one sort or another that have been neither difficult nor expensive to come by.

Where is the joker in the deck; or is there one? Isn't this the culmination of the ideals of widespread, adult, life-long education which leaders in the Adult Education movement have been praying for and writing, speaking and teaching about for years? Isn't this the direct and practical implementation of the philosophy of such benign cultural institutions as Britain's Open University and the Adult Education experiment by television that taught so many Italians to read and write ten or so years ago, as well as the implicit aims of those much-heralded visionaries who once reserved TV channels for educational purposes back in the early 1950s, to say nothing of the rhetoric of the foundation pundits who have been plugging something they have called "Public" or "Educational" TV for twenty years?

In a way, of course, it is exactly this culmination and realization of their dreams, and, in terms of the involvement of masses of people, it probably comes far closer to their best idealistic objectives than current broadcast TV, home study courses or Adult Education classes in schools and colleges. It produces, however, a nagging problem, of absolutely no concern to denizens of corporation suites, advertising agencies and even—sad to say—most (but not all) foundation oracles, whose function in life is to spend as much money as quickly as possible on causes that cannot be faulted by the Internal Revenue Service either as non-altruistic or non-up-lifting.

The great hazard boils down to a simple (and possibly inevitable) eventuality: that videocassette Adult Education will emulate exactly the broad pattern of conventional Adult Education, except to spread it more widely, trivialize it even beyond its present state and make its surface attractions even more interesting to the general public than they are at present.

Make no mistake about the matter: a small, hard core of that which is offered *right now* under the rubric of Adult Education *is the real thing*—that is, the serious investigation, by adults and their teachers, into the sustained development of adult talents, into significant issues and attempts at the honest expansion of life's dimensions by the diligent and careful study of one or another aspect of the arts, sciences, crafts and skills that have been neglected either in the participant's previous education, daily life and/or occupation. It is this kernel of genuine education—by no means confined only to official Adult Education curricula offered by legitimate schools and colleges—that may be placed in jeopardy by the Adult Education boom that the video-cassette industry is competent to destroy or severely damage. If it *does* destroy it, the loss will be a sad one, even though such destruction will affect a mere fraction of the adults presently engaged in so-called education, because most of them, as we have seen, are already involved in trivia and nonsense and might as well be watching televised situation comedies.

A hazard is not a tragedy, however, and a loss is not a cataclysm. Hazards may be prevented, and losses may be anticipated. So may be the probable nature and direction of the application of videocassette technology to Adult Education, as we observe the direction the wind blows today. Because such enormous potential financial gains are involved, it will be difficult to "head 'em off at the pass," as they say in Westerns, but many serious advocates and enthusiasts of Adult Education lack neither determination nor nerve.

The practical problems involved seem, at first glance, insoluble in a free market place filled with all manner of software manufacturers, free-lance educators and confidence men. But the solution is, in fact, quite simple. It requires, first, prescience and second, organization—*before* the technology of videocassettes inundates the consumer market, as it will—that is, soon, or, in other words, now or tomorrow morning.

First, collusion is necessary—collusion between the Adult Education Association of the United States (and Canada) and its various satellites, two or three of the giant foundations (that have been wasting their millions on fools' missions in this area for decades), a half-dozen large universities and—possibly—the Department of Health, Education and Welfare of the United States Government and its opposite number in Canada.

If professionally prepared, first-rate videocassettes (or videocassette reproduction services) of Adult Education courses *in any subject a grownup is likely to be seriously interested in* (yes, even including consciousness-expanding, improving one's sex life or building ships in bottles) are offered to the public *at cost*, and if *proper academic credit is given freely to those who complete such of these courses that are*—in any construction of the term—*academic,* and if the cassettes are prepared by the best talent available (not necessarily recruited from the educational world but from among the business, entertainment and professional communities as well), the trivialization of Adult Education by a glut of videocassettes and their hucksters is likely to be halted before it starts. In other words, private entrepreneurs, public fakers and the presently established "continuing education" fakes (whether connected with certified schools and colleges or not) will be eliminated from the game at the start. And it is possible—just possible—that so powerful a central body as this collusion requires (offering its wares almost free) can prevent the low-common-denominator tendency that has both permeated and directed almost *every other* mass technological innovation during the past fifty years.

A conspiracy or combination in restraint of free trade? Possibly, but so are our systems of free, public education for children. Does not its philosophy apply equally as aptly to adults? Is this an armchair dream that will be fought tooth-and-claw by the owners of the present software junk (publishers, broadcasters, conglomerates, etc.) waiting in the wings to unload the entire corpus of it into the videocassette market? Yes, a dream, of course, portending exactly the kind of battle that those very same foundations and educational bureaucrats who tucked Education Video under their wings twenty years ago won without a fight. Armed with their grants and millions, their do-goodism left both the public and the schools with a twenty-year record of failure to make good the promises of Educational Broadcasting, resulting in the present feeble Public Broadcasting Network currently in the throes of chaotic identity confusion. (Corporate profits to RCA, CBS and ABC have at no time in the past two decades been touched or placed in jeopardy by *any* large foundation grant to educational broadcasters of *any* kind, nor are they at present—a major symptom, and possibly one major cause, of the blatant failure of ETV, ITV and PTV in the United States.)

The main question that such a brave move raises centers on what kind of fibers the serious phalanx of our Adult Educators today is made of. They have for many years been enmeshed in an on-going cultural catastrophe, not of their own making and about which they could do little. Video-cassettes represent a potential liberation from this bear trap, possibly the first and last such opportunity they will be offered in the foreseeable future. Adult Educators have behaved in the past like frightened, waltzing mice, because they have had to; their constituency has responded best and most avidly to the worst and least worthy wares that they have had to offer. Now they have an opportunity to act like men—and like educators. They will *not* accomplish this end by an *entente* with non- (or anti-) educators in the world of commercial software and among the professional culture merchants. If they stand up and take what is rightfully theirs—the eyes and ears of adults who want to learn but do not know the options open to them or what real learning entails—a new era in Adult Education may erase the sins of the past and replace kind impulses with honest virtues and a record of accomplishment in opening the blessings of growth and accomplishment to those who may *need* it less but *deserve* it more than children—our adult population.

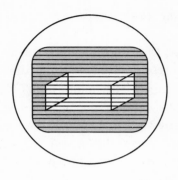

CHAPTER NINE

VIDEOCASSETTES AND SPECIAL EDUCATION

Estimates by the United States Office of Education hold that twenty-four million Americans eighteen years and older are functional illiterates. In addition, it is estimated that eight million to twelve million children now enrolled in school are headed for functional illiteracy. This functional illiteracy is not only to be found in the black slums, the rural South and Appalachia, but in virtually every school district in the country, whether it be rich or poor. So widespread and alarming is this handicap, that when the late United States Commissioner of Education, Dr. James E. Allen, assessed the condition, he chose literacy for everyone as the nation's major educational goal for the decade of the 1970s.

One of the problems in trying to standardize and achieve such a goal in public education is the diffusion of efforts, standards and teaching methodologies among the twenty thousand local school districts in the country.

Relatively little is known about the exact processes of the eye, ear and brain—how they coordinate in relation to the individual's learning to read. Thus, theories of teaching reading abound, as do the arguments concerning the merits and demerits of the various methodologies.

Software producers of videocassettes have facing them an unprecedented challenge and an opportunity in this area of special education. They will have to choose among methodologies of teaching reading. Our prediction is that they will go all major ways to protect their investments—that is, videocassettes will be made to support and sustain the phonics method of teaching reading skills, the "look-say" method of teaching reading, *and* the mix-method of teaching reading skills (a combination of phonic and "look-say" with proportionately varying degrees of each method in order to court local preferences). One would expect little innovation on the part of videocassette software makers in the field of reading-skills teaching. Experience leads us to believe that the exploration of existing methodologies will be the norm in order to achieve the widest sale of the software.

The matter of teacher preparation will also be a field for the videocassette software producer. It has been found that young teachers are confused about how best to teach reading. Publishers of teaching materials, in order to satisfy all contending factions and to protect their investments, have opted for materials that mix various approaches. Video-cassette makers have an opportunity and a challenge here, and, who knows, they may strike a rich vein.

There are few educators who challenge the view that given good teachers, good methods and a well-conditioned and controlled classroom environment, it is in the early grades where much of the best formative work in teaching reading can be done. Instruction will assure greater success where the teacher, working with small groups of five to ten children, can give individual attention to each child. The videocassette may be of immense value here to both the teacher and the child, supplementing, enriching and reinforcing the development of reading skills.

Of particular importance will be the classroom use of origination equipment by the teacher tailored especially to the reading dysfunction of the student. If the handicap happens to be a form of dyslexia, the teacher can and should be able to produce special remedial videocassette software with the proper medical guidance to treat the child and supervise his remedial progress. This means that originating equipment should be simple and easy to operate in situations which are *physically* difficult for the teacher. Cameras should be self-adjusting and practically automatic in their operation aside from a simple trigger and/or push-button mechanisms to initiate and stop the operation. Tape threading for videorecording must be automatic, one of the most exciting promises made by videocassette technology today. There is also the possibility that the student himself may operate the camera, the tape and the accompanying audio pickup. His own origination and playback will probably, in many cases, add further motivation and perspective for him to overcome his reading handicaps.

The cassette may also be used to help retrain improperly prepared teachers who are already on the job. Thus, a series of postgraduate retraining courses, for credit, with remunerative and promotional incentive, might be created by videocassette makers working closely with experts in the field, with the promise of a substantial market. Many educators have pointed out that similar retraining played a major role in upgrading the teaching of science, mathematics and foreign languages under the National Defense Education Act of 1958. This, the educators point out, should be accompanied by better diagnostic aids in identifying those children who have reading problems that are the outgrowth of physiological and psychological problems.

This, of course, brings us into the major category of special education that is at once poignant and heartrending, imperative and demanding. It is the education of those children (and adults) whose work is impeded by some physical or mental handicap. In this area, videocassette software makers have specific targets to aim at—the crippled, the blind and the partially sighted, the deaf and the hard of hearing, and defective in speech, the children of low vitality, the mentally retarded and the "behavior problems." And some educators also include here the gifted children.

Most sentient educators know well that there is a large number of handicapped children who need special education, and that far too few are receiving it. The special education that these handicapped children are receiving is, for the most part, found in the larger urban and more affluent suburban areas. The less seriously handicapped are often overlooked. Educators, in general, agree that the common aim regarding the education of the handicapped is to prepare them to lead lives successfully in contact with those who are not handicapped. What is needed is adequate vocational guidance and training, with placement and follow-up services in each case. More and more is being done to help develop the special aptitudes of the handicapped child. This is often done in special classes in the public schools and in special schools for various types of handicapped children. Advantageous to success in educating the handicapped is early discovery, treatment and training.

It has been estimated that there are somewhere between four and six million children in elementary schools alone in the United States who require special education. In some estimates, this does not include the malnourished, whose ranks may easily double the figure. To some people, special education is mere charity. Thus, educating the blind, the crippled, the emotionally disturbed, the hard of hearing and the sickly, they argue, should be relegated to specialized education in special schools financed somehow by the parents themselves. Many such schools have sprung up across the country. Yet the magnitude of the problem and the human values involved are such that, if each handicapped child could be educated to reach his or her full potential, society at large would be the immediate beneficiary in all respects.

At one time, the education of the blind, the deaf, the feeble-minded and the delinquent was almost exclusively the province of the state and private schools. Local public schools carried no responsibility in this difficult and expensive area. The partially sighted, the hard of hearing, the defective in speech, the emotionally unstable, the less seriously mentally retarded and the child of lowered vitality were admitted to the public school. More often than not, they simply failed in their school work. This was considered inevitable. Slowly, the concept of prevention crept into the training and education of such children.

Concepts such as home instruction, remedial treatment, vocational training and placement were not considered specific responsibilities of the public school. Contrast this older view with current advanced thought in many educational circles. Here we quote from a recent announcement from the American Telephone and Telegraph Company:

> If a child can't go to school, maybe the school can come to her. A child who gets ill or has an accident can miss weeks or months of school. [One who is permanently handicapped can miss a lifetime of school, we add.] Since visiting-teacher programs cannot match the hours of instruction provided in classrooms, home-bound students often fall behind.

Now there is a special telephone system to help children keep up with their studies, while they recover. It's called Tele-Class. It's being used in a number of cities.

In Oakland, California, for example, all the child needs is a telephone, a headset, the right textbooks, and a specially trained teacher like Molly Steele.

Mrs. Steele used to teach regular elementary school. But now she has a class of ten children. Some ill at home, some in the hospital.

She assembles her class by telephone. She can talk with all the children, and they can talk among themselves.

But at the touch of a button, Mrs. Steele can talk with any student privately. She can also divide the class up into discussion groups. So the children get a classroom atmosphere complete with the give-and-take of discussions and the stimulation of question-and-answer sessions.

They also get twenty hours a week of education they probably would have missed before.

So much then for the temporarily handicapped. Such systems can and should be utilized nationwide for the *lesser* temporarily handicapped. If such a device could be combined not only with the special teaching talents of a Mrs. Steele, but also with other teaching talents trained for special situations to aid handicapped students and recorded by the software videocassette people for distribution, what a rescue operation it might prove to be! We calculate that the initial investment in hardware and software would be repaid in full many times over not only to the investor, not only to society at large, but also in the humanitarian sense, to the afflicted children and to their often distraught families, in a matter of months.

Where inadequately trained special education teachers might prove a stumbling block to such a system, the distribution of special teaching talent by videocassette, with or without the use of telephone lines, to special classrooms, to special schools, to homes, to institutions and to hospitals for the variously handicapped could prove vitally effective in their educational process. And the individual tailoring of the cassettes to each characteristic handicap could readily be accomplished—at nominal cost.

Not all handicapped children and adults will benefit from using origination equipment in making their own videocassettes, but under the proper circumstances, such equipment may aid immeasurably in the recovery and/or the retraining and/or the basic training processes. Specially designed origination equipment for those physically handicapped to the point where they are unable to handle normal origination equipment may not prove to be a profitable enterprise at present for hardware makers or for educators, for many reasons. However, here is an area of experiment and inquiry into which one of the many foundations in America might well turn some of their charitable monies, for design development, distribution and training in the use of videocassette technology. The handicapped person (under proper guidance, educational and medical) would thus make himself the subject of his *own videocassette.* He might be able to see and assess his handicap in a new, objective and, as yet, unexamined light. It would be possible for him to keep a historical videocassette-file on his own progress in dealing with his handicap with the possibility of discovering new hope and concrete encouragement from it if, in reviewing his own file, he is able to ascertain on videocassettes irrefutable evidence of his own progress against his handicap.

A further word should be added here in regard to special

education. Not only should such education include care, instruction, placement and follow-up practices, but the prevention and the arresting of the handicap's affliction should also be attacked. This probably would necessitate a nation-wide program against disease, poverty, ignorance and fear itself that dooms so many partially handicapped individuals to social roles as pariahs, far more incompetent than, in fact, they are.

One other special type of rare handicap is that peculiar possession of the gifted child: genius. Educators figure that there are between one and one-half million and two and one-half million gifted children among the fifty-one and one-half million elementary and secondary school children in the United States. If such children are not challenged and directed properly, they often become restless and bored with the sluggish and soporific pace of the traditional classroom education. Often, they turn mischievous out of boredom. Many of these gifted youngsters become problems and display peculiarly frustrating behavior. Many drop out of school at various levels and never live to realize their potentials.

Under a Congressional mandate, the United States Office of Education recently issued a report whose theme is summed up by the following quote: "Intellectual and creative talent cannot survive educational neglect and apathy." The report recommends that the gifted child, in order to achieve his potential, should be put into a flexible learning environment—"a differentiated educational experience" that is a combination of various class and teaching techniques, the ideal being individualized instruction. Rapid progress and enriching educational techniques may be used for such children; new subjects for in-depth and for widening study can be employed as techniques for the gifted. Often, in the larger school systems, special classes and special schools may be created for them. In all the above instances, the videocassette can be an almost ever-present educational tool.

Here, especially, the gifted can make good use of originating equipment for self-expression in complex and innovative ways in much the same way that young movie-makers have experimented with the art of film production. Learning at their own pace, they may even construct their own lessons and find and express new concepts and new relationships between pre-prepared videocassettes as they proceed at their own individual pace, in teams or alone. The videocassette is a natural vehicle for accelerated learning pace. And originating equipment can easily reinforce and further motivate creatively inclined students towards a more fruitful expression of their natural gifts.

Videocassette software manufacturers may take advantage of the needs for the special education required by the handicapped if they realize that the field is vast and requires a major effort on their part to fill a crying and, as yet, largely unmet need. The cassette programmer in particular should realize that, in smaller communities and in rural areas, the handicapped do not yet as a rule receive the best education for the fulfillment of their potentials. Cassette software makers can take guidance from the fact that most educators feel that for practically every type of handicapped child there should be some contact with normal children. Cassette software makers should realize that present educational practice recommends that as far as possible the child's attention should be directed away from his handicap to the development of his major possibilities and to the discovery and development of his special aptitudes.

The various categories of handicaps are not defined with precision, for what in one district might be considered a

handicap is sometimes not so considered in another. Generally, the crippled child, in the orthopedic sense, is one whose
handicap in bones, muscles or joints interferes with normal
functions. Education for such crippled youngsters falls into
various modes: special schools, special classes in regular
school buildings, country schools combined with boarding
homes, transportation for the children when travel is possible, classes and bedside instruction in hospitals and convales-
cent homes and home teaching in its various forms. In all of
the above, physical care, academic education and vocational
training are a three-pronged aspect of schooling. Through
physical care, one hopes that the child will return to normal
living as rapidly as possible. Skill in teaching these children
involves a background in child psychology with an added
insight into the emotional and intellectual significance of the
physical defect. The teacher will be helped if she understands
the child's physical treatment and prognosis. Often the child
must be protected from the cruelty and neglect of his own
family. The special school must secure the intelligent
cooperation of the child's family. Much use may be made of
the cassette for children so handicapped. The cassette may
accompany or substitute for the visiting teacher, and can
expand the world of experience with intense interest for
them and for others handicapped but not entirely bedridden.

The problems of partially sighted children are several-
fold: there are those with progressive eye difficulties who
may be harmed by regular school attendance; there are others
who have static low vision; there are those who have vision
impairment and cannot properly use their eyes. Often the
partially sighted, finding themselves in classes with normal
children, drop back and finally leave school. If they receive
educational training to fit their respective handicaps, they
often do well. Putting them into a school for the blind is

seldom the answer. Their educational progress must be suited to their handicap.

The partially sighted youngster may make use of the videocassette where repetition and scale of image on a large, bright screen can readily be controlled. Also, an imaginative use of the audio track to complement the video image can be of considerable help. Where the impairment of the vision is progressive, care must be taken not to aggravate the eye condition. Cassette software should be designed not only with the consultation of educational specialists, but also with that of medical and psychiatric personnel in order to best reach the education goals despite the handicap. Origination equipment should also be designed under the same conditions, when it is judged that the use of such equipment will be helpful to the child's progress.

A visual acuity test by a competent ophthalmologist will help in ascertaining the degree and kind of sight handicap a child suffers from and the severity of the educational process through which he can be put. Large, clear pictures without detail generally should be a part of the sight-saving classes, constructed so as to minimize the work-load put on the eyes. However, by no means need children be deprived of illustrative materials. Children with static eye conditions will probably be able to make more use of illustrative materials than those with progressive eye conditions. Education may continue for this handicapped group, in general, through the college level and beyond. Specially trained teachers are important for this group of children.

In cases of children with more than one handicap, the more serious affliction should be considered first. That is, if one is mentally retarded and partially seeing, the retardation should first be considered. Then the vision impairment should further temper the educational procedures in line with competent medical and psychiatric advice and guidance. Wherever possible, the partially sighted should join the normal class when vision is not called into play. Where vision is important, children with vision handicaps are best segregated into a class for special instruction. The videocassette can help the child normalize his educational progress and realize his fullest potential in an efficient and effective way. Manufacturers here need the guidance and consultations of specialists in the field.

Deaf youngsters are usually categorized as those who were born deaf, those who became deaf in childhood before language and speech were learned, and those who had insufficient time to understand speech and language as deafness set in. Many educators feel that deafness is a greater disability than blindness.

Diagnosis and treatment of the deaf and the hard-of-hearing are first steps in the process toward an adequate education. The use of hearing aids, where they will help, and the ability to lip read and to communicate with others by means of hand language are next steps. The main danger here lies in misunderstood and undiagnosed cases of deafness and hard-of-hearing in the young. Such children often spend years in public and private schools, working a little, writing some, idling away a good deal of the time, unengaged, losing interest in school and sinking into a lethargic state resembling feeblemindedness. If the discovery of deafness is made in time, the child may be given new life.

Many special schools teach by oral methods and by speech and lip reading. Others use signs as a means of instruction in that it facilitates the communication of ideas for any failure of the child to learn speech. Some schools teach by finger spelling or the manual alphabet. The deaf child begins his education without either speech or language.

He is thus usually five years or more behind his normal peers. His mental or comprehension gap may even be more of a handicap.

Here the videocassette maker may be of infinitely great help. Software can aid the student in acquiring the fundamentals of language and speech, and perform, tirelessly, rote procedures that would cause a live teacher fatigue and boredom. It can also assist in building up a functional vocabulary. Once language and speech foundations are set, the curriculum that is essentially the normal one may be enhanced and reinforced by proper cassette software. Academic and vocational education can proceed at a pace normal for comprehension.

There is another class of handicaps in children that could respond favorably to early diagnosis and treatment and into which the videocassette might fit educationally—the group of children with speech defects. These disorders are grouped into such subdivisions as stuttering or stammering, articulatory defects, disorders of the voice and aphasia. Stuttering is a disturbance in the rhythm of speech. Articulatory defects render the child's speech indistinct and usually include lisping, lalling, cluttering and nasality. Disorders of the voice are failures to produce smooth vocal tones of sufficient audibility. Aphasia includes failure of the child to make instant associations between and among the following: the hearing of a speech sound and the meaning of it; the graphic symbol of the sound; the articulation of the sound; and the writing of the sound.

Some specialists in children's education group those with lowered vitality into a distinctive class of the handicapped. They are those children who, because of some inherited or acquired disease, function in a listless manner with barely enough strength to keep up with their peers.

They are usually the children who have inherited or contracted tuberculosis, cardiac diseases, encephalitis, epilepsy, or those who are or have been malnourished. Other disease factors also enter the picture. Medical and educational personnel agree in general that, after early diagnosis and treatment methods, education, training and socialization—with stress upon ability rather than upon disability—is most desirable. The videocassette software makers may make the educational process more feasible for this handicapped group by presenting specialized materials for them beyond the means of the average school or school system.

In the case of the mentally retarded children, the problem is to find, diagnose and segregate them into special classes. This may help to prevent them from becoming completely discouraged through repeated failure in school. Software videocassette makers may enter the field when education tries to provide the type of training that will prepare them to engage successfully in unskilled or semi-skilled occupations. It is generally believed that about two percent of the children in our elementary grades are, in some measure, mentally retarded. This provides a wide field for those whose outlook on the problem is economic. Aside from these children, there are also teachers of the children to be trained as well as the education of parents who have to live with this all-too-frequently demoralizing problem.

Children who present behavior problems, those who have nervous disorders, or are pre-psychopathic or psychopathic make up an important and difficult segment of the school population. Often through ignorance, lack of care and cruel negligence, they are discouraged, failed and dropped out of school, and soon develop patterns of antisocial behavior that may become criminal. Caught early enough, treated with the full resources of medicine and psychiatry, given proper social guidance and educative exposure, it is believed that much productive humanity may be rescued from this derelict heap. All such behavior problems should be treated individually and as humanely as possible. The problem in education is to relieve the strains and tensions that come from the initially disturbing personality influences.

The anti-establishment behavior of the young (and the not-so-young) form a part of this pattern, often masking underlying deep-rooted illnesses. Primarily, the handicap about which we are writing here may be limited to the nervous, the emotionally unstable and the delinquent. Special schools, special classes and guidance clinics are preferable to juvenile delinquency institutes and prisons. If the video-cassette finds a way to enter into the educative process of these children, and we see no reason why it cannot, they may do this generation its greatest service.

Videocassette technology has a wide field of exploration and experimentation to enter where and when the education of the handicapped child is concerned. The opportunity is there. The economics are not prohibitive, even though the variety of handicaps seem to splinter and fractionalize the market. And, more important, one cassette may spark one child, and another Theodore Roosevelt or Helen Keller may be in the making.

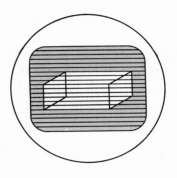

CHAPTEN TEN

A POTPOURRI OF PROPHECY

On one of his early visits to America, when he had already achieved world fame as a physicist, Albert Einstein was met at the New York dockside by the press and asked to explain his theories of Special and General Relativity. In a moment of lightheartedness, he said, in effect, that if we removed mass and energy from the universe, there would be no space and no time. Thus, he had underpinned the entire classical physics that preceded him.

To those who would prophesy, time is a sequential construct measured against human values. Underlying the act of prophecy are the questions: Where will man be tomorrow and the day after? What does the future hold for man? Does man have control of that future? Can he shape it to his design?

There have been many charlatans, many honest men, many deluded men, many inspired and informed men who have attempted to predict and predetermine the course of the future. Prophecy is an ancient trade, still practiced.

It is frequently prophesied that the seven thousand

items now on our supermarket shelves will soon disappear and that nine thousand new items will take their place; that pre-frozen foods made by the best chefs in the world will pass through fully automated kitchens and will fall into place on our dinner tables merely by the press of a button; that shopping will be done by television; that malnutrition will disappear from the world when edible sea and oil products appear on our dinner tables; that great cities will be built under the oceans and in the skies; that weather conditions will fall into the manipulative control of the hands of man in peace and in war; that recycling will save the natural environment from total pollution; that man himself will be taller and bald and have fewer teeth and that he will lose his little toe; that test-tube babies will be a reality and genetic medicine a new frontier; that population will be precisely controlled; that human organ banks will be a reality for transplants of all kinds; that complete and accurate computer and telephone diagnoses between doctor and patient will be possible; that cancer and heart disease will no longer be with us; that scientists will be able to selectively breed workers and leaders, geniuses and slaves; that drugs will give us controlled mental "trips" and expand or diminish intelligence; that robots and computers and other automated technologies will do most of our work and a good deal of our thinking; that life will be found in outer space and new horizons will thus open up for mankind; that modes of travel will include hydrofoils and personal pods; that the laser and maser beams will open up undreamed-of worlds, as will ultrasonics and atomic energy; that communications will occur by means of computer terminals and three-dimensional television in every home; that the world will be free of censorship; that the arts will express the new forms and values of life; that sex and the family will find new roles in society; that new religions will be born and old ones will be modified; that the family of man will be free from strife and racial problems; that cities will be controlled in size, form, shape, architecture and character; and that a new millenium is fast arriving.

All of the above will be achieved, we take it, through the advancement in technology, in science, in morality and in ethics; and passed on—how? Through education! There is the rub—through education. What can we predict about the indispensable instrument that will permit or destroy that future?

We might well and wisely paraphrase Dante here who, in the *Divine Comedy,* wrote of him who would predict, as he stood in Hell at the fourth gulf of the eighth circle, that those who would tell of the future have their heads fixed backwards on their necks as suitable punishment for their insanity and vanity.

How is all this Elysian prophecy to be accomplished? If it *must* be funneled through the process of education, then prophecy indeed tells us we are in trouble. Everett Reimer tells us in his book that *School Is Dead,* as he condemns today's educational system. The alternatives he offers in learning methods may prove as groundless as his prophecy.

The two fashionably "hip" authors of the pop-slick best-seller, *Teaching As a Subversive Activity,* advocate and prophesy a need for a new education, triangulated somewhere between McLuhanism, General Semantics and psychedelia. The traditional classroom has a false security to it, Postman and Weingartner claim. Can anyone trained in it survive in our cataclysmic society? What is needed, they prophesy, is a new education that will induce an "inquiring," "flexible," "creative," "innovative," "tolerant," "liberal" personality who can face uncertainty and ambiguity—in short, a modern demiurge. Thus, they advocate "inquiry learning," where history, instead of constituting a body of facts, becomes a tentative version of encounter therapy. In this odd notion of "inquiry learning," where once the American school system was established to teach benign acquiescence, the system will now engender healthy dissidence. This puts into direct conflict what the authors consider the rights of students and the universal practice of institutionalized education. What these authors overlook is that repression and conformity have been part (but only part) of *every* educational system as far back as history is recorded. Where and when few leaders have indeed revolutionized educational institutions, change has come mostly through the information and values imparted *within* the structure of the schools, rather than through the machinery or matrix of the educational institutions themselves.

Educational technologists have created countless *dei ex machinis* to supplement, to complement, to enrich and at times to replace the classroom and the teacher. Chalk and the blackboard, the eraser and the teacher's voice have become unfashionable in the educational-technological revolution of the past twenty years. Educational technology has been seized upon as one of the main panaceas for the problems of mass education. It has been argued that this is the best way to bring the best of teaching by the best of the teachers to the most students most economically. Oettinger, in his book *Run, Computer, Run,* foresees the use of computers in education that can diagnose the student's need, provide him with lessons and adjust the instruction to match his performance. Private corporations and government have financed experiments in televised teaching and in computer-based "systems approaches" to education. Prospects have not, by and large, been very spectacular. But software rarely lives up to its promise. And the hardware, oversold by its manufacturers and its advocates, usually finds itself stored in the basement with other obsolete technology, perhaps because it was and is too cumbersome, too difficult and too expensive to use.

Educational writers, such as Holt, Friedenberg, Goodman and others have condemned the schools as places of joylessness, designed to produce conformity and destroy the pleasures of learning. Perhaps no educational technology, no matter how imaginatively designed and used, will overcome this inevitable institutional lethargy.

Caleb Gattegno, in his book *Towards a Visual Culture,* advocates (along with many others) the use of television as the new instrument of effective and impacting teaching. This, too, of course, has yet to be proven in its widest ramifications. Many a television receiver in school classrooms throughout the country has been relegated to the audio-visual storage room. Gattegno believes that the child seeing for himself learns more and better than he does by means of the old methods of teaching in which the teacher merely tells him about something he is to learn. But most of the above assumptions have yet to be fully tested despite the glut of experiments already performed with ITV, few of which are convincing enough for common-sense detractors.

There have been many movements in American education that found their impetus in trying to free the child from the regimentation of the classroom. "Let the child learn by his own strategy and at his own tempo" about sums up the impetus behind most of them. Deformalizing the intellectual structure and loosening the content of the discipline into a kind of informal, individualized, creative adventure is advocated. Such philosophical rationales became the basic thrust years ago of progressive education in America. Holt and

others are going through a modern phase of this progressivism.

To begin with, it seems that we can accept the
hypothesis that cure will become more effective as diagnosis
becomes more accurate. This assumes that the art of healing
will keep pace with the art of diagnosis. This is not always
the case. For instance, medical doctors are quite sophisticated in the technique of diagnosing cancer of the blood.
Cures are still only in the "promising" stage. Holt's prophecy
as to why children fail and how this can be prevented is only
partially correct. His treatment will palliate only those cases
in which he is coincidentally correct.

If authoritarianism and structurally oriented school
systems were the only villains in the case for children failing
in school, then Holt and the entire group of which he is but
one might make a good argument for the type of child-
oriented school which he advocates. Then, of course, the
child would not be forced into the stratagems Holt describes.
Fear, the aberrations of competitiveness, self-protective,
obsequious behavior, feigned intelligence, and stratagems
aimed at pleasing adults might disappear from the classroom,
and the child might be forced to pursue the path of
self-fulfillment. The child would do those things in school
which would please the child. This might make school a
pleasurable environment rather than the oppressive one that
Holt (and group) say it is to so many children. His
child-oriented school, built to allow the child to study what
he wants, not in the progressive sense, which he considers
coercion coupled with kindly persuasion, but in the Holt-
sense as he describes it, wherein the child is "not pushed
around," would prove more ideal in an ideal society.

What happens to the child in our society when he gets
to school? He is confronted with a teacher whose chief means

of communication is via human speech, to which he is often unprepared to respond satisfactorily. If the child is allowed to study what he wants, as most school reformers are now advocating, he will, in all probability, avoid anything that is remedial for his major and critical educational problem. Since practically all teaching, from kindergarten through the post-doctoral level, leans heavily on human vocal communication and response (and will continue to do so even or especially in the child-oriented school), it seems that we can prophesy a lucrative field of programming for videocassettes. With the help of experts or superior teachers from their own school systems, students on a one-to-one basis with videocassettes can be brought up to maximal response to vocal communications both in the preschool years and in school. *Sesame Street,* the well publicized PTV preschool video program, may provide others with guidance in this direction—less stridently and more artfully, we hope.

Another aspect of the child's failure in school stems from the child's relationship to his parents, in that the desire of the child is to be proud of the parents and to imitate them. Lower-class parents may exhort their children to work hard in school, but these children do not see their parents in a role of intellectual or social mastery. Prowess in school is simply not a way of being similar to their parents nor of gaining adult resources of power that their parents possess.

Perhaps another bit of prophetic projection is in order here: If, by means of the videocassette in the home, adult orientation to positive cultural values can take place, the activity would be simulated by the child via the videocassette both in the home with the parent and at school as well. A public broadcasting videocassette production and distribution system directly into the home for adult education might prove a good start in this direction.

Reports have reached us that the big city high school is primarily "the trouble school." It is often too large to administer; it is chaotic, lost in bureaucratic mazes and educational wastelands and inhabited by delinquent children and demoralized teachers. The answer to this charge might be the mini-school, an experiment which is now being tried in New York. The mini-schools, which are still part of one high school, are organized around a common content theme, such as creative arts, aviation, urban affairs, etc. In addition, each group pursues a core curriculum of English, social studies and mathematics. The grouping is in a cluster of classrooms with an informal student-teacher lounge at the center. Students and the teachers spend their day in their respective corners of the big building.

The aim of this form of internal decentralization is to convert each of the mini-schools into an informal specialized alternative high school, where student-teacher relations are close and informal and where students are fired by their interest in the specialty in which they are working. Hostility and distrust between the students and teachers seem often to disappear. The prophecy here is that instead of the students and teachers travelling in a large, impersonal schoolhouse, teaching aids such as videocassettes are transported from mini-school to mini-school. Here is a fertile field for exploration of the utilization of special talents and interests of both students and teachers stimulated by videocassette technology.

Prior to relating videocassette technology to the future of American education in general, let us put the videocassette in its proper place: It is simply a storage and retrieval system for software (a fancy euphemism for one or another kind of audio and video experiences); origination equipment is that technology which stores words and pictures, usually on tape, so that they can be played back at will as frequently as one desires; playback equipment allows the tape videocassette (or possibly film or discs) to be played back through a slightly modified normal television set; a videocassette is a pair of reels that feed and rewind videotape; this tape is enclosed in a flat, but somewhat bulky, container; it may be inserted into an appropriate record and/or playback device with a minimum of fuss and bother, most particularly *without threading.*

There is little question that some form of videocassette technology will be widely used eventually in education—and in government, business and the home. Too many large international corporations have invested too much money for the videocassette industry to remain dormant too long. We also predict standardization relatively soon of two or three presently competing systems for the economic stability of this industry at large. One finds precedent for this prediction in the standardization of 1/4 inch audio recording tape, in the field of record-cutting where the 33 1/3 rpm microgroove disc also became the standard displacing the 78 rpm and outdistancing the 45 rpm record at the same time that the small audiocassette produced yet *another* standard for recording and playback, to say nothing of the 8 track stereo cartridge!

Interchangeability among the various systems of video-cassette technology is desirable and will be possible (as it is for audio technology) in the foreseeable future. This will allow cheap and quick copying or reproduction of video-cassettes and facilitate mass distribution of prefabricated videocassettes, mainly, we think, to home markets. The growing sophistication of origination equipment will allow for easy production of home-made videocassettes and almost inevitably for the emergence of an "underground" industry in such videocassette duplicating as there now exists in the record and audiotape business.

Also, this origination equipment will allow for individualization and limited distribution of specialized videocassettes. We predict that, just as there is now a style in film making called *cinema verite*, a new style of *tape verite* will emerge in high schools, colleges and in our culture at large. In fact, it has already been born. The instantaneous record and playback, the capability to wipe and reuse the videotape and the further sophistication of electronic editing of videocassettes *without touching the tape* are its present and future strengths. The erase and reuse aspects of videotape will allow for the continual up-dating of all educational videocassette software on the local level and thus give it a strong economic and educational advantage over both film and videodisc recording. Specialized programs for specialized audiences will and may be produced economically and easily. Thus, in the future of videocassette tape technology we see a more dependable technology than either film or disc, easy to handle, and economical to maintain.

We predict color will serve as more than a novelty in the future uses of the videocassette but an integral part of its aesthetic. We predict that portable, transportable and stationary videocassette machinery will find its way into homes, offices, schools and into other institutions. In most instances, control equipment for origination, record and playback technology will be foolproof and nearly automatic. In professional applications, such as in open broadcasting and in cable television, controls will remain manually operated in order to achieve the ultimate in precision.

Videocassettes will be able to freeze frame, print-out, split frame, chroma key, function in high contrast as well as low contrast lighting indoors and outdoors, and will be able to be electronically edited with exactly the precision with which film is now edited. With mass production and distribution, the prices of the technology will, we hope, drop to reasonable levels, permitting videocassette technology eventually to be found in almost every home in America, as are the radio, the telephone, the television and the record player today. Videocassettes will eventually be able to record up to several hours of materials at a standardized 3/4 inch tape width (as we see it and guess) in the near future—and color recording will eventually be no more expensive than black and white recording. The standard videocassette will use tape, not film nor disc forms, have two sound tracks for special effects and overdubs and, of course, one control track—hence our faith in the 3/4 inch format.

What impact will it have on American education and its problems, as treated above? Probably no more and no less than the film, the record player and the television set have had to date. And these devices are yet to be fully and fairly assessed. This we are most certain of: that the educational problems videocassette technology solves (if any) will be replaced by new educational problems it creates, just as *all* technology eventually creates an unforeseeable fallout that often takes years to surface. For the fact still remains that we know very little about how the human mind functions and grows and how the human being learns. There is, as yet, no universal training or learning theory in our competing psychologies, and videocassette technology is unlikely to provide us with evidence or experience upon which to build one. Hence, it will take its place in our evolving educational technology as a useful, but not the ultimate, instrument in training, learning and teaching whatever we consider worth imparting to the next generation.

And so with our heads on backwards, as Dante fancied, we have stood for a moment in Hell at the fourth gulf of the eighth circle and brewed a potpourri of prophecies. All of this, of course, is predicated on Einstein's thesis that mass and energy do not disappear from the universe, taking with them all space and all time, including videocassettes and TV tubes.

Envoi

The accompanying chart has been constructed at the urging of our publisher, who lives in the sweet belief that if a diagram or chart can be constructed of anything, that *anything* must be (a) clarified and (b) truer than it was before the thing was charted.

Here was the exact sort of situation that the great Pole, Copernicus, found himself in as he pored over the volumes of epicycles that had, over the centuries, been added to correct Ptolemy's colorful but incorrect construction of how the solar system worked. "There must be a better and/or simpler way to do this!" one can almost hear him protesting. And when Copernicus discovered the absurdly simple solution to his problem—heliocentricity—it frightened him so completely that he hid his findings and lived out his days fiddling with his charts pretending ignorance of his genius.

Our particular chart was constructed in the early part of 1972, a period roughly analogous, we think, to the founding of the Roman Republic in relation to Copernicus' experience. Like Ptolemy's original design, it has been based upon observation, what we have been told and what we have read in the fanciful literature of videocassette technology moonshine and public relations releases at this period of its development. It is, we think, *reasonably* accurate—or was yesterday—but it is also likely to be highly deceptive, because, like Copernicus' documents, it too has been the victim of countless epicycles (or corrections) that have reached our desks almost daily for the past two or three years.

As a chart, it is somewhat like a Racing Form as well, replete with significant information about the contests to be run at the track but genuinely meaningful only to the initiated and frequently irrelevant to what actually happens when the bell sounds and horses start running. (For this reason, the best course we recommend for a novice at the track is to find someone *else* who seems to be winning a lot of money and bet on the horses that he favors.)

As a skeleton key to this particular document, let us therefore try to cut through some epicycles and offer our opinion as to who the winners will ultimately be in the videocassette and cartridge confusion the chart actually indicates:

Eastman Kodak's entry into this field is, first of all, critical to the future of all kinds of videocassettes. Eastman has already, of course, moved well into the 8mm and Super 8mm cartridge field for films utilizing optical resolution. It is now but a short step for them to *add* electronic resolution instrumentation to their present line, and they will have—for all practical purposes—probably edged out all other film or non-magnetic systems from the videocassette field. Whether this move on the part of Eastman was and is the reason CBS, in fact, threw in the sponge on EVR remains entangled in corporate secrecy, just as its effect upon the disc systems and the projected RCA plastic software system is also, to date, a mystery.

We are, therefore, left with the various magnetic tape systems—the only devices on the chart which provide for instant replay origination as distinctive from conventional film cassettes and cartridges. Now, the question arises as to what type of tape will be used in these systems and whether they will take the form of cassettes or cartridges.

The answer to the question is that it really *does not matter very much what is inside of a cassette or cartridge*; the important factor is what it *does.* The tape is not touched, nor are the reels handled. And tape width or size, the number of reels involved, etc., are quite unimportant from the consumer's viewpoint. From the technical viewpoint, we believe that Sony's 3/4 inch tape cassette will become an industry standard, for many reasons. But, if a way is found to use 1/2 inch tape in the same manner as 3/4 inch tape (with sufficient control and sound tracks and electronic storage capacity), what conceivable difference will it make to the consumer if the latter is used, except that the cassette involved will be 1/4 inch thinner? (At the present writing, Matsushita Electric of Japan—Panasonic to its friends—is developing the 1/2 inch magnetic tape line with the same avidity that Sony is working on the 3/4 format.) The same principle applies to Avco's Cartrivision system, the video-cartridge system that, we believe, at present, offers the best and most economical possibilities for the *home* market, just as the 3/4 inch (or 1/2 inch) videocassette systems will probably meet most educators' needs best. Avco seems to be headed in the direction of manufacturing complete videorecord systems (home entertainment centers that may be operated in many modes for CATV reception, conventional VHF and UHF-TV recording, showing "movies" and so forth). Sony (and its followers and imitators in Japan and elsewhere) seems more interested in developing and marketing *components* of full systems, such as cassette players, duplicators, stop-frame mechanisms and similar items that may be integrated one way or another into older systems, or may take advantage of the Japanese tendency to standardize the individual components and connectors of competing equipment, regardless of the manufacturer.

But the unexpected may always be expected in technology. And our conservative predictions may fly with the wind by the time you read this. Word has just reached us (by carrier pigeon) of a new system handled by the Videorecord Corporation of America which utilizes a *card* (sic) of "4 x 5" inches in size, upon which, somehow, thirty minutes of video and sound material may be stored and replayed. Isn't that nice? Where would *it* fit on our chart?

Then, there is Creative Cine-Tel, Inc., that claims it offers optical movies displayed in hotel rooms, employing an instrument that projects moving pictures and sounds stored on 70mm film in a way that boggles the mind! And let's not forget Tenavision, Inc., that displays *something* in the privacy of motel rooms, or Sensory Devices, Inc., Computer Television, and so forth, and so forth and so forth—including Motorola, which may or may not be sticking by CBS' discarded EVR system and hurl itself into the electronic greatness.

Why don't we all return to this chart, say, in about ten years and—if health sustains—have a hearty laugh over it. Humor derived from what we once took seriously is the only guaranteed appreciative speculation on the market today.

VIDEOCASSETTE AND CARTRIDGE CAPABILITIES

Names	Compatibility and Standardization	Recording Potential	Cost of Playback Equipment	Cost of Recording Medium	
MAGNETIC TAPE: (1/2 inch or 3/4 inch tape) Ampex (Instavision); Avco (Cartrivision); Japan Victor; Panasonic; Philips (VCR); Sony (U-Matic); 3M Company		YES (Instant)	MEDIUM TO HIGH (about $800-1200)	HIGH	1 →
FOIL OR PLASTIC DISC: AEG-Telefunken (Teldec Video Disc)	No possibility among the several systems except for Sony and 3M, who have agreed on 3/4 inch tape format (Panasonic has a 1/2 inch tape cassette) Possibility exists, however, that sub-components like video monitors and control mechanisms may be standardized	NO	LOW (about $180-$420)	LOW	2 →
CBS/Motorola (EVR—in suspension)		NO	HIGH (at present, $800+)	HIGH	3 →
Nord Mende (Vidicord) Eastman Kodak (8mm and Super 8mm cartridge) etc. Polaroid (self-developing)		YES (with 8 or Super 8mm camera)	MEDIUM TO HIGH	MEDIUM	4 →
RCA (Selectavision) Holographic plastic or film; RCA also showing some interest in magnetic tape videocassettes		NO	MEDIUM TO HIGH ($600 projection probably conservative)	LOW TO MEDIUM	5 →

VIDEOCASSETTE AND CARTRIDGE CAPABILITIES
(Continued)

s (inued)	Video Picture Quality	Reliability of System	Ratio of Playing Time to Duplication Time	Cost of Duplication of 12 copies	Cost of Duplication of 500 copies	
NETIC TAPE: nch or ch tape) ex (Instavision); (Cartrivision); Victor; onic; s (VCR); (U-Matic); ompany	No single system has an inherent substantial picture quality advantage over any other using broadcast standards as a reference	AVERAGE	Less than 50 to 1	LOW	MEDIUM	1→
OR TIC DISC: Telefunken ec Video		VERY GOOD FOR SINGLE DISCS	Greater than 1000 to 1	VERY HIGH	LOW TO MEDIUM	2→
Motorola R—in suspension)	In practice, however, there appear to be differences in quality among the devices as the result of different research and development techniques	AVERAGE	Less than 50 to 1	HIGH	MEDIUM	3→
Mende cord) nan Kodak n and Super cartridge) oid developing)		AVERAGE	Less then 50 to 1	HIGH	MEDIUM	4→
ctavision) graphic plastic m; RCA also ing some interest agnetic tape ocassettes		PROBABLY AVERAGE	Less than 50 to 1	PROBABLY VERY HIGH	MEDIUM	5→

VIDEOCASSETTE AND CARTRIDGE CAPABILITIES
(Continued)

Names (Continued)	Cost Dup. 10,000 copies	Ability Erase Reuse Record Medium	Playing Time	Single Frame Storage Potential	Video Playback Pickup Method	Major Market Control	
MAGNETIC TAPE: (1/2 inch or 3/4 inch tape) Ampex (Instavision); Avco (Cartrivision); Japan Victor; Panasonic; Philips (VCR); Sony (U-Matic); 3M Company	HIGH	YES		YES (with allied equipment)	Helical scan mag. head pickup	Consortia of U.S., Japanese and European electronics firms	1
FOIL OR PLASTIC DISC: AEG-Telefunken (Teldec Video Disc)	VERY LOW	NO	All systems may, one way or another, achieve equivalent playing time Video Discs are limited at present to a few min. per disc Teldec has identified a changer pack that, they claim, will provide only momentarily uninterrupted long-playing performances	NO	Pressure pickup	AEG-Telefunken + Decca of London (the latter concerned with software)	2
CBS/Motorola (EVR—in suspension)	HIGH	NO		YES	Flying spot scanner pickup	CBS conglomerates (including software interests, now waning)	3
Nord Mende (Vidicord) Eastman Kodak (8mm and Super 8mm cartridge) etc. Polaroid (self-developing)	HIGH	NO		YES (with modified equipment)	Flying spot scanner or vidicon pickup	Nord Mende Eastman Kodak	4
RCA (Selectavision) Holographic plastic or film; RCA also showing some interest in magnetic tape videocassettes	Probably MED. TO LOW or LOW	NO		Probably YES	Laser and vidicon combination pickup	RCA (including software interests)	5

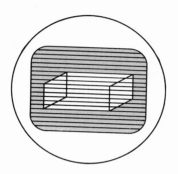

REFERENCES

Aserlind, L. Audiovisual Instruction for the Mentally Retarded. *Audiovisual Instruction,* 1966, *11,* 727-730.

Barr, Donald. *Who Pushed Humpty Dumpty? Dilemmas in American Education Today.* New York: Atheneum, 1971.

Barzun, Jacques. *Teacher in America.* Garden City, New York: Doubleday & Co., 1954.

Baumgartner, B.B. *Guiding the Retarded Child.* New York: Day, 1965.

Bell, Daniel (Ed.) *Towards the Year 2000.* Boston: Houghton Mifflin, 1968.

Brown, Claude. *Manchild in the Promised Land.* New York: Signet Books/The New American Library, 1965.

Clark, Ronald W. *Einstein: The Life and Times.* New York: World Publishing, 1971.

Conant, James B. *The Comprehensive High School.* New York: McGraw-Hill, 1967.

Cremin, Lawrence A. *The Transformation of the School: Progressivism in American Education, 1876-1957.* New York: Vintage Books/Random House/Knopf, 1961.

Cremin, Lawrence A. *The Genius of American Education.* Pittsburgh: University of Pittsburgh Press, 1965.

Cruickshank, William M., John B. Junkala and James L. Paul. *The Preparation of Teachers of Brain-Injured Children.* Syracuse: Syracuse University Press, 1968.

Dewey, John. *The Child and the Curriculum.* Chicago: University of Chicago Press, 1902.

Dewey, John. *The School and Society.* Chicago: University of Chicago Press, 1900.

Ellingson, Careth. *The Shadow Children.* Chicago: Topaz Books, 1967.

Eurich, Alvin C. (Ed.) *Campus 1980, The Shape of the Future in American Higher Education.* New York: Delacorte Press, 1968.

Falk, Irving (Ed.) *Prophecy for the Year 2000.* New York: Julian Messner, 1970.

Gattegno, Caleb. *Towards a Visual Culture: Educating Through Television.* New York: E.P. Dutton, 1969.

Genensky, S.M. Some Comments on a Closed Circuit TV System for the Visually Handicapped. *American Academy of Optometry,* July, 1969, *46*, (7), 519-524.

Glasser, William. *Schools Without Failure.* New York: Harper and Row, 1969.

Goodman, Paul. *People or Personnel.* New York: Vintage Books/Random House, 1968.

Gordon, George N. *Classroom Television.* New York: Hastings House, 1970.

Holt, John. *How Children Learn.* New York: Pitman Publishers, 1968.

Holt, John. *How Children Fail.* New York: Pitman Publishers, 1964.

Illich, Ivan. *Deschooling Society.* New York: Harper and Row, 1971.

Jencks, Christopher and David Riesman. *The Academic Revolution.* New York: Doubleday, 1968.

Kahn, Herman and Anthony J. Weiner. *The Year 2000.* New York: Macmillan, 1967.

Karlsen, B. *Teaching Beginning Reading to Hearing Impaired Children Using a Visual Method and Teaching Machines.* University of Minnesota, United States Office of Education, Project 1204, 1966.

Kozol, Jonathan. *Death at an Early Age.* Boston: Bantam Books/Houghton Mifflin, 1967.

Money, John (Ed.) *Reading Disability.* Baltimore: Johns Hopkins Press, 1962.

Oettinger, Anthony G. *Run, Computer, Run: The Mythology of Educational Innovation.* Cambridge: Harvard University Press, 1969.

Perkinson, Henry J. *The Imperfect Panacea: American Faith in Education, 1865-1965.* New York: Random House, 1968.

Piaget, Jean. *Science of Education and the Psychology of the Child.* (Translated from the French by Derek Coltman.) New York: Orion Press, 1970.

Platt, John Rader. *The Step to Man: A Striking Collection of Visionary Essays on the Evolving Social and Intellectual Nature of Man.* New York: John Wiley and Sons, 1966.

Postman, Neil and Charles Weingartner. *Teaching As a Subversive Activity.* New York: Delacorte Press, 1969.

Reimer, Everett. *School Is Dead.* New York: Doubleday, 1971.

Ridgeway, James. *The Closed Corporation: American Universities in Crisis.* New York: Random House, 1968.

Rosenthal, Robert and Lenore Jacobson. *Pygmalion in the Classroom: Teacher Expectation and Pupils' Intellectual Development.* New York: Holt, Rinehart and Winston, 1968.

Saettler, Paul. *A History of Instructional Technology.* New York: McGraw-Hill, 1968.

Silberman, Charles E. *Crisis in the Classroom.* New York: Random House, 1970.

Taylor, Harold. *Students Without Teachers: The Crisis in the University.* New York: McGraw-Hill, 1969.

Timpano, Doris M. *Crisis in Educational Technology.* New York: Gilbert Press, 1970.

Viscardi, Henry. *The School.* New York: Eriksson, 1964.

Wagner, Rudolph R. *Dyslexia and Your Child.* New York: Harper and Row, 1971.

Recent Videocassette Sources
(caveat emptor)

Anonymous. Cartridge Television (special section). *Billboard*, September 26, 1970, c1-c16.

Anonymous. Cassette TV Goes International: U.S. Eyes Teldec Video Disc TV. *German American Trade News,* October, 1970, 4-7.

Anonymous. Sony Begins Videocassette Production. *Business Management/Engineering,* November, 1971, 27-29.

Anonymous. The TV Networks Shrug Off New Competition. *Business Week,* March 27, 1971, 90-96 (esp. p. 91).

Klein, Stanley. TV Cassettes: A Look Ahead. *New York Post,* February 4, 1971, 41.

Lauchenbruch, David. The Videoplayer Era. *TV Guide,* January 16, 1971, 6-10.

Also note the monthy report, *Video Cassette Newsletter* (Martin Roberts and Associates, Inc., Box 5128N, Beverly Hills, California 90210); *VidNews* newsletter (Billboard Publications, 165 West 45th Street, New York, New York 10036); as well as the now (reportedly) quarterly magazine *Videorecord World* (Playback Publishing Ltd., Urbanus Square, 2418 MacArthur Boulevard, Newport Beach, California 92660). Also, the minutes of *The First International Cartridge TV, Videocassette and Videodisc Conference* (eight booklets from Special Projects Division, Cardfront Ltd., 7 Carnaby Street, London W1, England, a subsidiary of Billboard Publications, Inc., U.S.A.).

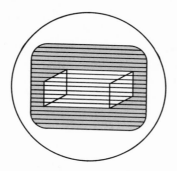

INDEX

Date Due

Due	Returned	Due	Returned
MAR 15 1989 FEB 15 89			